Reverse Mission

Religion and Politics Series

John C. Green, Ted G. Jelen, and Mark J. Rozell, series editors

Reverse Mission

Transnational Religious Communities and the Making of US Foreign Policy

TIMOTHY A. BYRNES

Georgetown University Press / WASHINGTON, D.C.

Library of Congress Cataloging-in-Publication Data

Byrnes, Timothy A., 1958-
Reverse mission : transnational religious communities and the making of US foreign policy / Timothy A. Byrnes.
     p.   cm. ———(Religion and politics series)
Includes bibliographical references and index.
ISBN 978-1-58901-768-9 (pbk. : alk. paper)
   1. Catholic Church—Latin America. 2. Catholic Church—Political activity—Latin America.
3. Catholic Church—Foreign relations. 4. United States—Foreign relations—Latin America. I. Title.
   BX1426.3.B97 2011
   261.7098'09045—dc22   2010048162
ISBN 978-1-58901-775-7 (casebound edition)

♾ This book is printed on acid-free paper meeting the requirements of the American National Standard for Permanence in Paper for Printed Library Materials.

15 14 13 12 11   9 8 7 6 5 4 3 2   First printing

Printed in the United States of America

For Molly

Contents

Preface

I have been thinking about the transnational dynamic that forms the heart of this book for a very long time—the entirety of my scholarly career, in fact. During graduate school at Cornell University more than twenty-five years ago, I had the distinct privilege of working on a research project with two of the great figures in the study of US foreign policy: George McTurnan Kahin in my own government department and Walter LaFeber in the (then) neighboring history department. President Ronald Reagan had taken office a few years before, promising to halt the spread of communism in "America's backyard," and by the spring of 1985 newspapers and political journals were full of speculation that American involvement in El Salvador was going to turn into another Vietnam. Taking advantage of having at my disposal one of the country's foremost experts on the US experience in Vietnam (Kahin was just publishing *Intervention*, the culmination of a lifetime of study of US involvement in Southeast Asia) as well as a great diplomatic historian who had just published a book on the US role in Central America (LaFeber's *Inevitable Revolutions* was justifiably receiving a great deal of attention at the time), I decided to find out if all of this speculation had any validity. So under the able direction of Professors Kahin and LaFeber, I spent a fascinating semester comparing President Reagan's policies in El Salvador in 1983 with President John F. Kennedy's policies in Vietnam in 1963. What I found was that the similarities were numerous, profound, and deeply troubling. Words like "counterinsurgency" and "third way" had dominated policy debates concerning both countries in both eras, for example. And although Reagan's team had learned not to use the loaded phrase "domino theory," their fears about a "loss" of El Salvador that would lead to the inevitable radicalization of Central America and Mexico were direct echoes of all of the talk in 1963 about Vietnam being the first step in a grand communist conspiracy that would ultimately threaten the independence of Japan. The white papers that were

ix

produced by the State Department in both cases were virtual mirror images of each other. And in one of my most interesting discoveries I found that the personnel working on Central American issues in the Reagan administration were in many instances the very same people who had (mis)handled Vietnam for President Kennedy two decades earlier.

I considered turning that research into a doctoral dissertation on the continuities of US anticommunism, or even on the provocative observation that Reagan and Kennedy had brought such similar worldviews to the White House. But I was dissuaded from that path by two considerations. The first was that Kahin was nearing retirement in 1985 and was not taking on any other graduate students at that time. I am not sure he would have worked with me anyway, because unlike most of the doctoral candidates he advised, I was not an area specialist in Southeast Asian politics. But Kahin's impending retirement precluded a serious discussion of the possibility, and given that LaFeber was not a member of my department, the doors to further research on El Salvador and Vietnam appeared closed to me.

More importantly, however, I was distracted from any further examination of the many similarities I had uncovered concerning the policies in 1963 and 1983 by what I had found to be one of the most interesting and salient *differences* between the two cases. President Kennedy had been prodded in 1963 by the so-called Catholic lobby to reconfirm his opposition to a communist takeover of South Vietnam and throw ever greater US weight behind the misbegotten rule of its Catholic president, Ngo Dinh Diem. In stark contrast the only real organized opposition in 1983 to President Reagan's policies in El Salvador, including his strong support for President Napoleon Duarte, came from Catholic organizations, particularly American nuns who worked as missionaries across Central America.

Now *that* was an interesting finding, one that suggested a sea change in the political position of the Catholic Church within the United States and a significant development in how individual Catholics were conceptualizing their identities, their loyalties, and their political energies. I can still remember how interesting that development was to me at the time, and how enthusiastically I would have welcomed the prospect of spending the next two or three years expanding on that finding and thinking through its many ramifications for the role of religion in the making of US foreign policy. But one huge obstacle was in my way: I could not imagine that any faculty member in the government department at Cornell—or at any other major university, for that matter—would take such a project or prospect seriously at that time. I never even discussed it very much with my professors or shopped a proposal around to see if it would excite any interest because I presumed to know what their reactions would have been. Religion? Religion and foreign policy? Religion and international relations? These simply were not considered viable topics of study at that time, so I buried my questions about nuns and US foreign policy in a file drawer and went on to other topics.

As it turned out, I was lucky enough to find two members of the Cornell faculty who had taken note of the growing attention to religion in the subfield of *American* politics and who were therefore open to another idea my preliminary research had sparked: a dissertation on the role that the Catholic Church had played and was playing in domestic American politics. It was a big step from civil war in El Salvador to partisan cleavage in the United States, and my focus had to shift entirely from the passions of nuns to the machinations of bishops. But it was my chance to get a PhD studying an aspect of the relationship between religion and politics, so I leapt at the opportunity. Indeed, if I owe a debt of gratitude to George Kahin and Walter LaFeber for encouraging my early interest and giving me the first space to explore it, I owe even more profound thanks to Ted Lowi and Ben Ginsberg (now of Johns Hopkins University) for giving me more running room to explore my abiding interest in religion's intersection with politics than any graduate student had the right to expect in 1985.

That was more than twenty-five years ago, and in the ensuing years I have been able to sustain my interest in religion and politics and my focus on the Catholic Church. I finished and published that first study of bishops and parties; I spent a number of fruitful years studying other aspects of Catholic politics in the United States; and then through the good graces of a Fulbright semester in Poland and the reemergence of transnational politics as a branch of inquiry in the field of international relations, I was able to shift my interests and energies back to the role of the Catholic Church in world politics generally, and finally to the making of US foreign policy more specifically. At the same time, the field itself also shifted and grew in response to events. Phenomena as diverse as the rise of the Christian Right in the United States, the Catholic roots of Solidarity in Poland, and the inauguration of an Islamic republic in Iran brought religion back into the foreground of world politics and established a greater degree of legitimacy for the academic study of religion within the social sciences. There was, and still is, considerable secularist resistance to taking these events and developments seriously on their own religious terms; and "religion and politics" as a professional subfield still resides on the relative margins of my discipline of political science. But a tremendous intellectual space has opened up since I was first discussing Catholicism in the context of Vietnam and El Salvador with Kahin and LaFeber during the Reagan years, and so I find myself at long last drawn back to the original questions, albeit in somewhat different forms.

This book is not a comparative study of US foreign policy per se, nor is it an examination of the developments in transnational Catholic loyalties that have revolutionized the forms that Catholic political mobilizations take and the effects that those mobilizations have on policy. Instead, this book is a comparative analysis of three Catholic religious orders or communities and an examination of how the transnational structures of those communities serve as the indispensable foundation of the roles that they play in the making of American foreign policy. The Maryknoll nuns who first captured my attention through their opposition to President Reagan are here. But so are Jesuit priests who responded with outrage to the murder of six of their own by a Salvadoran military funded by the United States. And so are Benedictine monks in Vermont who established a lasting covenant with Benedictine nuns in Latin America and sought to use that covenant as a foundation on which to build a greater level of understanding and cooperation across the United States–Mexico border.

These three communities are similar in that they are all animated by transnational religious commitments that profoundly
shape the political commitments that they make as US citizens. But
the three communities—Jesuit, Maryknoll, and Benedictine—also
differ from each other in significant ways that profoundly affect
how they articulate their loyalties and advance their interests. Indeed, one of the central arguments of this book—and one I most
definitely would not have had the temerity to make in 1985—is that
the specific form of a religious community's political mobilization
is a direct function of the transnational structures and spiritual
commitments that animated it at its founding. More specifically,
when Jesuit priests try to influence US policy in El Salvador, they do
so as members of a tight-knit global order whose educational apostolate provides them with substantial institutional resources and
places them near the center of American social and political life.
In contrast, when Maryknoll nuns speak out against US policy in
Nicaragua, they do so as missionaries in a double sense: both to the
suffering people of Nicaragua and in a reverse sense to their fellow
citizens in the United States, whose attitudes and political stances
must be converted through greater knowledge of what is being done
in their name. And finally, when Benedictine monks seek to forge
closer bonds across the social, cultural, and economic chasms of
the north-south divide, they do so by embodying the Benedictine
principle of hospitality and by offering sanctuary in several different forms to people they see as being deeply harmed by the policies
of the US government and the complacency of the US population.

For me, one of the most interesting aspects of performing this
research was discovering that these structures and commitments
not only shaped the form that the communities' political mobilizations have taken; they also shaped the responses that the communities made to my requests to study them. Frankly, I had not expected
that form of congruence. But the more I experienced the varied approaches that these particular Catholics took to my questions and
inquiries, the more the approaches made sense to me. Every Jesuit
priest I asked to interview for this book, for example, agreed to meet
with me; and all of them, as far as I could tell, were comfortably
forthcoming in their answers to my questions. Most of these men

were my fellow academics, and a large number of them were college presidents. Their talks with me were straightforward conversations about timelines, events, and facts, as well as they could recall them. We met invariably in academic offices, with a desk separating interviewer and interviewee, and there was nothing much different between those encounters and all of the interviews I have conducted with Catholic bishops over the decades. This is how institutional leaders behave, and this is how institutional leaders convey their insights and experiences.

The contrast with the Maryknoll nuns could not have been more clear. Almost all of the women that I contacted over the course of this research also agreed to meet and talk with me. But they did so with a wariness that was clearly grounded in their hesitation to trust me to do justice to "the people" towards whom they still feel a powerful bond of loyalty even many years after the circumstances that they and I were discussing. These women were missionaries. They applied the values and methods of that particular vocation when they returned to the United States and worked tirelessly to evangelize their fellow citizens—not on the catechism, but rather on what they took to be the catastrophic effects of US foreign policy. But they also applied those values to their dealings with me. They met with me to tell the story of the people they had worked with. They did not fully trust me, but I came to see over time that they thought my book could play its own minor role in advancing what they called their "reverse mission."

I thought when I started this research project that the Benedictines would be the hardest community to study. The monks in Vermont and the nuns in Mexico are monastics, after all, and they live in relative isolation and insularity. Or so I thought. Both groups of Benedictines surprised (and pleased) me with their enthusiastic willingness to let an outsider into their communities for the purpose of better understanding the covenant that binds them together. In both cases a small group of members sat with me for formal discussion (three brothers in Vermont and four sisters in Mexico City), but it would be difficult to overstate the level of Benedictine hospitality the communities afforded me when I came to visit their houses. This is what Benedictines do, apparently—at least these particular Benedictines. And it was obvious to me from the start that the hospitality they afforded me in this work grew out of the same principles that drove their creation of a cross-border covenant and their commitment to north-south understanding.

It should go without saying (but I will say it anyway) that I could not have written this book if it was not for the trust and cooperation I received from the many Jesuit priests, Maryknoll missioners, and Benedictine monastics I spoke with and stayed with over the course of the research. I hope that I have been able to maintain the appropriate distance necessary to produce a relatively objective treatment of the political activities under examination. I certainly have been willing to be critical of these communities when I thought it was appropriate to be so. But I cannot claim that I have remained neutral in terms either of my reaction to the work that these good people do or of my personal regard for them as human beings. It was a privilege to be welcomed into the lives, work, and homes of these Jesuit priests, Maryknoll missioners, and Benedictine monastics, and I am deeply grateful to all of these communities in personal as well as professional terms.

I am also grateful to the many other people who assisted me over the course of the inexcusably long time I worked on this slim volume. Lil Mattingly, MM; Thomas Reese, SJ; Paul Fitzgerald, SJ; and Marie Morgan, MM, were among the many people from the religious orders who talked with me outside of formal interview sessions about the subjects covered in this book. Gene Palumbo was an informative and provocative guide in San Salvador, where Kevin and Trina Yonkers-Talz also welcomed me and introduced me to the inspiring students of Casa Solidaridad. I want to thank all of the people who shared time with me at the Guadalupe Center in Cuernavaca, Mexico, but especially the staff and students of Lees-McRae College who were there on a service learning trip under the auspices of their Global Community Center. They all showed great patience to the one participant in the experience who was also a questioning observer. Scott Crawford, Rebekah Graham Saylors, and Selena Hilemon were the Lees-McRae administrators accompanying the students on the trip, and all three were kind enough to let me talk with them about those observations as I was actually experiencing them. Rebekah also procured and delivered a CD that the Benedictine brothers and sisters had made about their *alianza*.

Speaking of university students, I am grateful as always to my own students at Colgate University who have taught me so much over the years as we have talked about transnational religious communities and their intersections with political processes and institutions. Much of what we discussed in classes on transnational politics and religion and politics serves as the theoretical background of what appears in this book. If any of these students read the book, I hope they will appreciate the role that they played collectively in clarifying my thinking and my analysis. Cindy Terrier, the administrative assistant of the political science department at Colgate University, is a steady and indispensable fixture in my professional life, and I thank her as always for all of her help and support. The faculty research council at Colgate funded most of the travel that was necessary for me to conduct the research for this book. Richard Brown of Georgetown University Press understood exactly what I meant when I told him that I wanted to structure this book around the stories that can be told about these religious communities, and he encouraged me and fortified me as I tried to make meaningful theoretical points in the context of narrative. The reader can judge whether I justified his trust in that regard.

In each book I have published over the years, I have always acknowledged my children for the blessings they have been in my life and for the great joy I have derived from being their father. I have also thanked them for being such genial and flexible traveling partners, and that certainly applies in this case. Brigid, my talented linguist of a daughter, accompanied me to El Salvador, where she served as seamless translator, delightful companion, and patient sounding board. Gavin stayed closer to home this time, but he was no less on my mind and in my heart as I finished this volume. My mother and father deserve thanks for all that they have given me over the course of my life, but most especially in this context for introducing me to the Benedictine brothers of the Weston Priory when I was too young to even understand what a monk was. That was quite an example of parental prescience on their part. Finally, this book is dedicated to Molly Ryan, whose support and love are indispensable to me in a million ways but whose direct effect on *Reverse Mission* was mainly to delay its completion. The reason is simple: Being with Molly always seemed more fun and more compelling than anything that work had to offer.

CHAPTER 1

Transnational Religious Communities and the Making of US Foreign Policy

- A Jesuit priest in California's Silicon Valley agrees to drop everything and take over as academic vice president of the Universidad Centroamericana (UCA) in San Salvador when that Jesuit university's entire administration is murdered in cold blood by the Salvadoran military. At the same time, many other Jesuits in the United States devote themselves to halting US financial support to the Salvadoran military and insist that the murders at the UCA be properly investigated and aggressively prosecuted.
- A Maryknoll sister, who is spending her life in Nicaragua, travels back to the United States to speak at public meetings, where she insists that President Reagan's "freedom-fighting" contras are actually terrorizing the people that she and her fellow missioners have gone to Nicaragua to accompany in their suffering.
- A group of Benedictine brothers in Vermont joins a group of Benedictine sisters in Mexico City to open the Guadalupe Center in Cuernavaca, where visitors from the United States can be introduced to the reality of Mexican poverty and to the role that their own government's foreign policy plays in perpetuating that poverty.

1

These three circumstances have a number of important things in common. First, in all three cases US citizens took concerted action to influence US foreign policy in Latin America. The targeted policy was very specific in the case of the Jesuit priests, somewhat more general in terms of the Maryknoll sisters, and rather diffuse when it came to the Benedictine monastics. But in all three cases members of close-knit religious communities expressed solidarity with their religious brothers and sisters who live outside the United States, and they engaged in political mobilization and political activism for the purpose of changing US foreign policies that were antithetical to the interests of those brothers and sisters. Moreover, the styles of mobilization and forms of activism that these US citizens chose to pursue, in all three cases, closely matched the particular structures of the individual religious communities to which they belonged and grew directly out of the particular religious missions to which those communities were committed.

The Maryknollers have a wonderfully descriptive name for this kind of transnational feedback loop within their own community: They call it reverse mission. Sent out into the world to spread the word of God and to accompany the poor in their suffering, these missioners view the consciences of their fellow US citizens, and the policies of their own US government, as appropriate mission territory as well. The particular form that reverse mission takes in the case of the Maryknoll sisters comes directly and specifically from their experience as missioners abroad, but surely the phrase can apply equally well and usefully to all three of the cases that I have listed above and will be discussing throughout this book. "Reverse mission," as I use the phrase here, refers to any process through which members of religious communities speak in the United States for their brothers and sisters living abroad who, though profoundly affected by US foreign policy, have no political platform in the United States from which to speak for themselves.

These Jesuits, Maryknollers, and Benedictines engage in reverse mission in very different ways, according to their own traditions and their own community's practices. But as we will see throughout this book, they all do it for very similar reasons. These US citizens speak and act on behalf of members of their particular communities who reside abroad because at the most fundamental level, all of these priests, sisters, and brothers have chosen to define their personal lives in terms of transnational religious identities. These members of religious communities, in other words, speak out about US foreign policy and try to change it, not only because of opinions they hold, but also at a deeper level because of who they are—because they are US citizens with close communal ties to citizens of other nations. The forms that those ties take, and the degree to which they are voluntary and chosen, may be unusual. But the fact that the ties exist—and that they motivate US citizens to act politically on the basis of *who* they are rather than by *what* they want—places the members of these religious communities well within an important stream of contemporary American political life.

The political scientist Harold Laswell famously said that politics is about "who gets what, when, how."[1] In our own time, however, we might add to Laswell's classic definition the idea that politics is also about *who* we are and which communities we belong to. We are living in an era characterized by identity politics; and an awful lot of energy is expended, not to mention blood spilled, over questions involving membership, allegiance, and identity. Categories like race, gender, sexual orientation, and religion have come to reside at the very center of our politics. As a result, politicians are often defined as much by who they are, and which segment of the population they purportedly represent, as they are by what they say or how they propose to solve the nation's problems. In a similar way policies and interests are often defined in terms of who the likely beneficiaries are and whether a given group of people has a legitimate right to make claims on the basis of its specific collective identity.

One of the most interesting things about identity, in both personal and political terms, is just how complex and contingent it is. Just as we might be, at one and the same time, members of families, practitioners of professions, and fans of sports teams, so we can also be simultaneously citizens of countries, members of ethnic groups, and devotees of religious traditions. Moreover, as contexts shift and change, the particular political communities that inspire our allegiance also change, sometimes dramatically. This is certainly true in terms of religious affiliation. For much of American history, after all, religious affiliation was one of the defining features of American demography and was therefore a central element in shaping American political identities.[2] People in the United States were classified as "Protestant, Catholic, or Jew"; and whichever category one fell into, it was usually a clear indication of the specific political community one lived in and even a remarkably reliable predictor of one's partisan affiliation and voting behavior.[3] Phrases like the "Catholic vote" and the "Jewish vote" denoted an American population wherein religious designation had real political meaning and in which the members of any given religious community could be assumed to have generally consistent political interests.

In our own day these time-tested connections between religion and politics have been powerfully altered by the twin effects of diversity and secularization. The American population is much more diverse in the twenty-first century than the old categories of Protestant, Catholic, and Jew could possibly capture. And many Americans now want nothing to do with the personal religious identities of their parents and grandparents. That is not to say that religion no longer plays a role in formulating political identity in the United States. Even a cursory glance at the modern Republican Party reveals that the ties between religious affiliation and political identity are still strong.[4] But for a certain subset of Americans in our own era, religious affiliation now serves as a kind of *alternative* or *complementary* political identity derived from membership in *transnational* religious communities that stretch well beyond the boundaries of the United States of America. In short, a powerful sense of shared "we-ness," to cite an awkward but illuminating term, binds many Americans to their coreligionists in other parts of the world. And that sense of shared identity—an experience that many people define as a mutual commitment of solidarity—might under certain conditions encourage those Americans to think of themselves and of their status as US citizens in complex religious terms, rather than in straightforward national ones.[5]

This commitment to transnational solidarity is precisely what can make religious affiliation so controversial in the context of US domestic politics, particularly in terms of foreign policy. US citizens who band together with foreigners as coreligionists and try to influence US foreign policies in terms of that religion are often subject to charges of dual loyalty and insufficient patriotism at best, and national renunciation and treason at worst. Jewish Americans have long felt the sting of this charge in response to their support for the state of Israel, and controversy still surrounds the so-called Israel lobby and the degree to which it exerts influence on US policy in the Middle East.[6] These days, and especially since 9/11, American Muslims face a kind of pervasive mistrust concerning their loyalty to the United States. In some ways the burden of proof has been placed on members of the Islamic faith to demonstrate that they are sufficiently devoted to American interests abroad and that they are not members of some kind of vast sleeper cell of religion-based disloyalty.[7]

For their part American Catholics have fought long, hard, and successfully against the canard that they are beholden to a "foreign potentate" in Rome and therefore are insufficiently exclusive in their devotion and loyalty to the United States of America.[8] After more than two centuries of loyal service to American causes, foreign and domestic, one rarely hears today the kind of doubts and distrust of Catholics that sunk Al Smith's candidacy in 1928 or that challenged John F. Kennedy's in 1960. Indeed, Catholic politicians today—candidates for national office like the late Geraldine Ferraro and more recently John Kerry and Joe Biden—are more likely to be criticized by their fellow Catholics for being insufficiently obedient to their religious tradition than they are to be denounced by non-Catholics for being overly subservient to it.[9] Most American Catholics, in other words, apparently mesh their multiple identities with relative ease.

All that said, however, I focus in this book on an important aspect of the relationship between Catholic identity and US citizenship, an aspect that is as understudied and overlooked as it is theoretically interesting and potentially influential. I am referring to the powerful bonds of community and solidarity that link many American priests, brothers, and nuns with their religious brothers and sisters in other countries around the world. These men and women are not laboring in some un-American thrall to a mysterious (and suspect) "Pope of Rome." But these particular Catholics belong to what their Church calls religious orders or congregations; and the ties that bind the members of these communities to each other can be, and indeed usually are, very strong. As David Ryall has phrased it: "It is the religious orders and congregations that are the transnational elements within the Church, operating as they do across national boundaries and answering to their Rome-based superiors."[10]

Most members of these orders join them at rather young ages, and through a process known as "formation" they are educated and socialized according to the principles and practices of their individual communities. These men and women live, work, and pray together. They grow into adult maturity with each other and generally internalize together a powerful set of assumptions about the community itself, about the members' responsibilities to each other, and about the role that their particular community or order should be playing in the world. This process of formation is a lifeshaping and lifelong process that powerfully brands an individual Catholic as, say, a Jesuit priest or a Maryknoll missioner or a Benedictine monk or nun.

This book is an examination of the political activities of these three Catholic communities: the Society of Jesus (Jesuits), the Maryknoll Congregation, and the Benedictine Confederation. Crucially, these Catholic communities, and many others like them, are deeply transnational in their institutional structures and in their religious missions. To be sure, much of the formation mentioned above takes place in a local or national context, and for most of these priests and nuns and monks their day-to-day contacts are with religious community members who are also compatriots and fellow citizens. But as we will see throughout this book, the identities that are formed and the loyalties that are engendered within these Catholic communities also weave a complex web of transnational connective tissue that very often supersedes the national boundary lines of international politics. The Spiritual Exercises of Saint Ignatius of Loyola, for example, form the spiritual foundation of all Jesuits, no matter where they may live. The Maryknoll ethos of mission similarly animates the lives of all Maryknoll missioners throughout the world and ties them deeply to the people they choose to accompany and serve. And the Rule of Saint Benedict structures the daily lives and practices of all Benedictine monasteries, no matter where they may be located.

Most United States–based members of these orders and communities harbor few doubts about their own identities as Americans or about to which country they owe their political allegiance as citizens. At the same time, many of these men and women also recognize that they owe an equally powerful communal allegiance to transnational religious collectivities that include members who are citizens of other countries—often other countries that are deeply affected by US foreign policy.

This set of religious and political relationships raises a number of analytical questions that I address in this book. To what extent, for example, does the transnational nature of these communities lead to political mobilization and policy advocacy on the part of the US citizens who belong to them? Can these political activities be defined credibly as efforts to protect or advance the interests of brothers and sisters in religious orders abroad or of the national populations to which these other members of the specific religious community belong? What actual effect, if any, do the avenues of communication and religious fellowship opened by these communities have on US policy towards specific countries? Put in the bluntest terms: Is this form of dual loyalty politically significant in any tangible sense?

These questions situate this research in the growing literature that reflects a resurgent interest in religion's role in world politics. A number of books have been published, for example, that address this question of transnational religious identity and its effect on world politics.[11] However, the very targeted focus of this book is actually motivated by my conviction that the best way to deepen our understanding of these phenomena is to study them in the very particular: to identify specific transnational religious communities and examine the ways in which those communities relate to individual countries and to the international state system in general. In short, I believe these Catholic orders of priests and nuns and monks command our attention as a kind of test case of transnational intrareligious mobilization in a globalized world, in which the bedrock of state sovereignty and the dominance of national identity are being challenged from many different directions.

Through examination of these cases—Jesuit, Maryknoll, and Benedictine—I make three related arguments. The first is that these religious communities do indeed exercise influence on US foreign policy. That influence may not always be conclusive, and at times it may not even be obvious or widely noticed. But I point to a number of instances where United States–based members of Catholic religious orders were able to shape and affect US policy in one direction or another. For the Jesuits that influence involved tangible effects on specific US policy. In the Maryknoll case the influence was less direct but perhaps no less important, in that it centered on the missioners' crucial role in constructing the political context in which important national policy debates took place. The Benedictines, not surprisingly, had the least direct and tangible effect on policy per se. The nuns and monks who are featured in chapter 4 focus their collective energies on building solidarity across international borders and on educating US citizens about what is being done in their name in Latin America. I define that kind of long-term political mobilization as at least potentially influential in terms of the formation of US foreign policy. But however one wants to define influence on policy—a notoriously difficult phenomenon to specify—my second core argument is that any meaningful political role played by these religious communities is a direct function of the transnational nature of the orders, congregations, and confederations themselves.

Jesuit priests, Maryknoll sisters, and Benedictine monastics differ from each other in significant ways. But what these three groups definitely share with each other is a powerfully formed sense of transnational identity that leads them to enter into the US policy process as US citizens, explicitly for the purpose of advancing the interests of members of these religious communities who live elsewhere. Finally, I argue that the evident variation in the forms that this advocacy takes is itself a direct function of the varied ways in which these orders define and embody transnationalism and of the varied ways in which they define for themselves their religious missions. To get ahead of myself a bit here at the beginning, I argue that Jesuit "contemplation in action," Maryknoll "mission," and

Benedictine "stability" and "hospitality" result in very different definitions of transnational community and lead to very different ways of participating in the processes of democratic politics in the United States of America.

Defining the Cases

In choosing the case studies to focus on in this analysis, I had a very common methodological decision to make. In one sense an emphasis on geographic and even denominational breadth in the case studies I included might have allowed me to draw correspondingly broader conclusions concerning the ways in which transnational religious communities are constructed and the ways in which those communities participate in political processes. At the same time, however, that same breadth of coverage would have also introduced into the analysis a host of extraneous factors and possibilities that might well have limited my ability to draw any sort of general conclusions from such a small number of cases. To strike the specific balance between depth of case analysis and breadth of analytical conclusion, therefore, I decided that all three cases would focus exclusively on the efforts of transnational *Catholic* communities to influence US foreign policy toward one specific region of the world, Latin America.

1. The first case involves Jesuit priests and their efforts to force the US government to respond more aggressively to human rights abuses in El Salvador. In 1989 six Jesuit priests, all officials or professors at the Universidad Centroamericana in San Salvador, were assassinated by the Salvadoran military. The US Jesuits who were sent to El Salvador to replace their fallen brothers at the UCA became leading figures in a coordinated effort to prod the US government (a) to pressure their Salvadoran allies to investigate and prosecute the murders more aggressively and (b) to reassess the US government's very close relationship with the Salvadoran military.
2. The second case concerns Maryknoll sisters and their reaction to US support for the counterrevolutionary insurgency against

the Sandinista government in Nicaragua in the 1980s. This is
the case from which the book's title, *Reverse Mission*, is derived.
Maryknoll missioners who were posted to Nicaragua used that
descriptive phrase to capture the responsibility many of them
felt to return from the mission field to educate US citizens
about what was being done in their name to the people, the
Catholic Church, and not incidentally the Maryknoll community in Nicaragua.

3. The third case examines Benedictine brothers in Vermont and
their spiritual, social, and political ties to their Benedictine sisters in Mexico. The Weston Priory is a small Benedictine community in rural Vermont whose monastic life is centered on the
strict prayer regime and manual labor mandated by the Rule of
Saint Benedict. In the 1970s the brothers of the priory established a close relationship, or *alianza*, with a group of Benedictine sisters in Mexico City. Over the ensuing years the brothers
have visited Mexico often, as they have immersed themselves in
the concerns, both spiritual and political, of their Mexican sisters. Those concerns are now a central part of the declared mission of the Weston community as the brothers seek to educate
themselves, their neighbors in Vermont, and their elected representatives about what they take to be the inequities of US policy
toward the state and people of Mexico. In the Benedictine spirit
of hospitality, the brothers and sisters have also opened a center
in Cuernavaca, Mexico, where guests from the United States are
encouraged to inform themselves concerning the social, political, and economic conditions of contemporary Latin America.

At their hearts these three cases are all iterations of the same transnational dynamic. The primary method of this book is to rely on a
close examination of these specific cases to shed light on the extent
to which, and the ways in which, that dynamic results in effective
political action by these three religious communities. However, I
have chosen these cases in such a way that their rigorous examination will also allow me to assess the impact of a whole host of other
potentially significant factors on the basic transnational dynamic
and political mobilization in which I am most interested. Those

factors, or variables, can themselves be grouped into three categories: (a) the sex and ecclesiastical status of each community's members, (b) the form and structure of each community, and (c) the way in which each defines its religious vocation and worldview.

First, the structures of the communities vary substantially in terms of both the sex and the ecclesiastical status of the individual members. The Jesuit community I examine here, both in the United States and in El Salvador, is made up of men who are ordained priests. The Maryknoll community, on the other hand, is made up of women who are professed sisters of their order but who, given the Catholic practice of ordaining men only, are obviously not ordained members of the Catholic clergy. Finally, the Benedictine *alianza* is an arrangement between two relatively autonomous communities made up of men in Vermont, most of whom are not ordained, and women in Mexico, none of whom can be ordained.

These structural variables of sex and status deserve careful attention. In methodological terms this is admittedly a small sample from which to draw meaningful conclusions. But it may well be that men and women have different ways of living in transnational community or defining transnational identity, just as the ordained and the nonordained may have different conceptions of their role in the Church, both locally and transnationally. Either or both of these factors could affect the way these communities translate their communal solidarity into group mobilization and political action.

Second, the basic forms that these three transnational communities take also vary significantly. The Society of Jesus, or Jesuit order, is a straightforwardly transnational entity that has members and communities throughout the world and that counts among its many roles the maintenance of educational institutions in the United States, El Salvador, and elsewhere. The Salvadoran Jesuits at the UCA and the US Jesuits posted to El Salvador after the killings in 1989 were brothers in the Society of Jesus, to be sure, but they were also professional colleagues devoted to the same transnational institutional aims. In contrast, the Maryknoll presence in Nicaragua is largely an American presence, one made up of women from the United States who have decided to travel to Nicaragua to live with and work for its people. Indigenous Maryknoll communities have been established in Nicaragua and elsewhere, but the order was founded in the United States and retains an American identity. The Benedictine brothers in Vermont and the Benedictine sisters in Mexico are members of a more loose-knit transnational religious community based on the substantial autonomy of individual monasteries tied to each other through their shared devotion to the Rule of Benedict.

These very brief descriptions are sufficient to indicate just how different the nature and form of transnationalism is in these three religious communities. These differences manifest themselves in very different modes of communal interaction, very different styles of political organization, and very different methods of political expression across the three case studies. Catholic transnational institutional organization is—not surprisingly, given the size and complexity of the Church itself—a remarkably diverse phenomenon.

Finally, the three communities define their religious vocations and specific worldviews in different ways. The Jesuits define themselves as "contemplatives in action," a phrase meant to capture a particular vocation based in the religious formation of Saint Ignatius of Loyola's Spiritual Exercises combined with an everyday pastoral and institutional style that is decidedly outward-looking. The Maryknoll sisters in Nicaragua, on the other hand, are missionaries. The concept of mission work has changed substantially in recent years, but these women from the United States still travel to other places as outsiders to advance the pastoral mission of the Church and work towards establishing conditions more compatible with their own conception of Christian charity and social justice. The Benedictines, finally, are a monastic order. The transnational Benedictine community is made up of men and women who are largely separated from the outside world in terms of daily life and who are devoted to the notion that disciplined prayer and manual labor ought to form the basic building blocks of their communal lives.

This last set of considerations is surely the least tangible of the three I have outlined, but it also may be the most provocative in terms of the book's basic aims. Here, as clearly as anywhere, the sacred confronts the secular directly. The concerted action of the Jesuit men, the missionary commitment of the Maryknoll women, and the contemplation of the Benedictine brothers and sisters result not only in very different definitions of transnational community per se but also in very different modes of transporting the discourse of the sacred to the secular world of political mobilization and policy advocacy. Different ways of confronting the sacred, we might say, result in different modes of negotiating the secular.

Since I am a political scientist by training and profession, however, I also approach these dynamics from the perspective of the analytical and theoretical categories of my chosen discipline. More specifically, I argue throughout my discussion of these three cases that the dynamic of reverse mission resides at a fascinating intersection of two evolving strands of inquiry in the field of political science: *foreign policy interest group mobilization* from the subfield of American politics, and *transnationalism* from the subfield of international relations. In my judgment, in fact, this particular intersection of these two strands presents a particularly fertile site for the exploration of what some have called the "desecularization" of contemporary politics.[12] Indeed, I believe that this particular intersection of transnational identity and national policymaking process is in many ways the very heart of religious politics in our time. Before I turn to the three specific cases that make up the heart of this book, therefore, let me first briefly introduce these strands of inquiry and illustrate the ways in which I combine them in the analysis that follows.

Foreign Policy Interest Group Mobilization

My discussion in this book of the political activities of American priests and nuns and monks who belong to transnational Catholic communities will intersect directly with a vigorous debate within the field of political science over the role of interest groups in the making of US foreign policy. Part analytical exercise and part normative admonition, this debate (or series of debates, more precisely) focuses on the degree to which interest groups *can* influence the making of foreign policy and (maybe even more frequently) on the degree to which interest groups *ought* to do so. To be sure, I will have occasion in the course of presenting these three case studies to report on opposition to the political activities of Jesuits, Mary-knollers, and Benedictines that is based on the normative claim that US citizens ought not to engage in political mobilization with or in defense of brothers and sisters outside the United States. By and large, however, I try to avert this normative thicket and instead focus on the analytical category of whether these priests and nuns do have an influence on policy, regardless of what I or my readers might feel about such an influence. Actually, my greatest intellectual interest in these matters concerns the institutional and procedural aspects of the circumstances—the way in which these very different religious communities embody transnational community, and the very different ways in which those communities articulate themselves politically in the context of making US foreign policy. But in order to address those procedural and institutional questions, I have to place them first in the context of the broader discussion of the groups' effectiveness and, to a lesser extent, of their propriety.

The first thing to note in any discussion of the role of interest groups in the making of foreign policy is that some leading strains of international relations scholarship do not credit domestic factors at all in this regard. What is generally called systems-level theory, for example, emphasizes the imperatives of "self-help" in an anarchic world and posits that state behavior is shaped and driven by the very nature of the system in which the states interact with each other. In a particularly influential formulation, Kenneth Waltz and his fellow structural realists have focused exclusively on structural variables—such as the number of major powers in the system—in their effort to account for the broad sweeps and trends of world politics throughout history.[13]

Not satisfied with this level of abstraction, or with structural realism's inability to explain why a particular state would take a particular action in a particular political context, another group of international relations scholars has chosen to emphasize the so-called domestic structures of individual states to account for the specific foreign policies pursued by states in world politics.[14] Generally focused on a broadly defined "strong state/weak state" continuum, this school of thought posits that the foreign policy of strong states—characterized by substantial governmental control of economic and social life—will be less beholden to internal political processes than will weaker states that are characterized by less governmental control and more vibrant civil societies. To put it in overly simple terms, foreign policymaking in Saudi Arabia is likely to be a markedly different phenomenon from foreign policymaking in Switzerland.

The United States is generally characterized in these discussions as a relatively weak state with a generally pluralist and open policy-making process. What David Truman once called a "multiplicity of access points" renders American policymaking a remarkably complex affair in which many elements and interests in society are able to participate.[15] Most relevant for our purposes here, however, is the common assumption that foreign policymaking is the least pluralist and least open aspect of American government. Civil society is undeniably robust in the United States, in comparative terms, and political life in Washington is indeed characterized by the dizzying array of interests seeking to gain access to the levers of power held by the three branches of the federal government. But the received wisdom on this question is that when it comes to the making of US foreign policy, government officials and a relatively narrow band of elites set the priorities and determine the specifics of government action relatively free of the influence of either public opinion or interest group contestation.

I say *relatively* free in this context, however, because while it is widely held that nonethnic groups tend to be unimportant when it comes to foreign policy, many scholars nevertheless argue that ethnic groups can and do often play a significant role in directing US policy abroad. Nathan Glazer and Daniel P. Moynihan may have overstated the case a bit when they wrote in their 1960s classic on the subject of ethnicity that foreign policy "probably [responds] first of all to the primal facts of ethnicity."[16] But they were not alone in their assessment that ethnic groups are powerful participants in the national debate—nor in their assumption that this is mostly a bad thing. As then Senator Charles Mathias (R-MD) put it in 1983, "the greater problem" is "the loss of cohesion in our foreign policy and the derogation of the national interest" when "factions among us lead the nation toward excessive foreign attachments or animosities."[17]

As I indicate above, this kind of normative commentary concerning the propriety of ethnic lobbying and the relationship between general American interest and particular ethnic interest gets much of the attention in both academia and journalism.[18] But a more important question for me in this book concerns the conditions under which this kind of lobbying is likely to be effective. Indeed, the very significance of the normative discussion itself is a function of the answer to the empirical question. If ethnic lobbies did not have any influence on actual policy, then it really would not be worth anyone's time to argue that they are illegitimate or dangerous. Cultural clubs and affinity associations pose no threat to American democracy.

My inclusion of this discussion in the context of introducing the role that religious communities play in shaping US foreign policy, of course, leads to the question of whether Jesuit priests, Maryknoll nuns, and Benedictine monks can really be analyzed in the same way as ethnic lobbies in terms of their participation in policymaking processes. Obviously, the transnational Catholic communities that interest me here are not ethnic in character, nor are they as broadly communal in nature as one might define a Jewish lobby or a Muslim lobby as being. These specific religious orders and communities are much more particular in their allegiances and identities than those broader categorizations might imply. But in his well-known examination of religious lobbying, Allen Hertzke emphasizes the significance of what he calls the "representation of foreign constituencies."[19] And after looking closely at these communities and the intensity of their transnational connections, I have come to believe that it is precisely the specificity and particularity of their allegiances and identities that makes the Jesuits, Maryknollers, and Benedictines so similar to ethnic lobbies in the approaches they take to the interests and concerns of their brothers and sisters in religious orders abroad.

The ties that bind Jesuits, Maryknollers, and Benedictines may not be on the order of the familial depth that might bind, say,

Armenian Americans with their relatives in the old country, or Cuban Americans with those they left behind on the island. But as we will see repeatedly throughout this book, the communal bonds that define transnational religious communities are nevertheless quite tangible and politically quite meaningful. As a matter of fact, I would definitely equate in intensity, if not necessarily in effectiveness, Jesuit outrage at mistreatment of fellow Jesuits with Irish American sentiment toward British rule of the Northern Ireland counties; Maryknoll insistence that US policy was harmful to the people of Nicaragua with Jewish defense of Israeli security; and Benedictine frustration at the plight of their Mexican sisters with Cuban American exhaustion in the face of Castro's endurance. One of my central claims in this book, in fact, is that the transnational solidarity I examine is really that fundamental, that motivational, that political.

In any event, Mohammed Ahrari performed a valuable service to everyone interested in these kinds of questions when he set out a template of conditions that do and do not augur well for ethnic influence on US foreign policy.[20] In so doing he provided a useful empirical foundation on which the normative debates can take place. But he also produced a set of categorizations that neatly define and explicate the kind of transnational religious solidarity that interests me here. Ahrari's first condition for successful ethnic lobbying is "the congruence of strategic interests promoted by an ethnic group and the U.S. strategic interests towards that group's old country."[21] Simply put, ethnic lobbies that are pushing through already open doors of US foreign policy are more likely to be viewed as effective, even if that effect is only to reinforce already well-established strategic interests of the United States. Ahrari cites this congruence as a central factor in the Israel lobby's reputation for effectiveness in Washington, for example. Speaking of American Jews, he says that "no other ethnic group in the country can claim such a substantial basis of harmony of strategic interests between its old country and the United States."[22] John Mearsheimer and Stephen Walt recently argued that this assumption of congruence is actually unwarranted and that the greatest success of the Israel lobby has actually been the establishment in the first place of that assumption of congruence of interests between the United States and Israel.[23] Regardless of where one might come down on that dispute, however, it is plausible to argue that factors such as Israel's vaunted status as the only democracy in the Middle East and its prominent support for American strategic interests during the Cold War make the job of Jewish supporters of Israel in the United States easier than the job of, say, Irish supporters of Ireland. The bedrock "special relationship" between the United States and the United Kingdom, after all, always complicated the ability of the US foreign policy establishment to respond affirmatively to the kind of "Brits out" demands that one sometimes heard in Irish and Irish American circles.

For their part, the particular interests of transnational Catholic communities often have complex points of intersection with US strategic interests as defined by American political elites. And those intersections often provide openings through which Catholic communities can seek to influence policy in ways that are advantageous to their memberships. Chapter 2, for example, is an examination of the efforts by Jesuit priests in the United States to reverse foreign policies that the Jesuits saw as hurting (to put it mildly) their brothers in El Salvador. In one sense, of course, the Jesuits' call for the US government to insist on an aggressive investigation into the murder of six Jesuits during the Salvadoran Civil War and also to halt military aid to the Salvadoran government ran directly counter to the strategic interests of the United States, as those interests were defined by the administrations of Reagan and George H. W. Bush. But in another sense, the arguments put forward by the Jesuits intersected directly with a debate that was occurring in those years between those administrations and their opponents in Congress about what American interests exactly *were* in Central America in the 1980s. A certain political space was opened in the context of that debate, and the Jesuits took up residence in that space to significant effect.

Ahrari's second condition for effective lobbying on the part of ethnic groups is "the degree of assimilation experienced by its members and the *implications* of such assimilation on the capability of group members to promote their foreign policy objectives in the US."[24] Again, Irish Americans present themselves as a counterexample. I would not argue that the Irish have played no role in the making of US policy toward their homeland. But I share Ahrari's conclusion that that role has generally been truncated exactly by the limited degree to which many Irish Americans actually experience their Irishness in politically meaningful ways, when compared these days to, say, Cuban Americans or Armenian Americans.[25] This matter of assimilation, by the way, has been a crucial factor in limiting Catholic influence as such on US politics and policy in both domestic and foreign contexts. There was a time, not so long ago, when "Catholic interests" could drive public policies on issues as diverse as film censorship on one end of the spectrum to support for a Catholic government in Vietnam on the other.[26] These days, however, most Catholics are so fully assimilated into American society that it might be as hard even to define a specifically Catholic interest in US foreign policy as it might be to advance one.[27]

It is true that the effects of assimilation are more obvious with American Catholics of European descent than they are with their Latin American coreligionists. Indeed, the Catholic Church in the United States still retains the possibility of playing the kind of political role within the Hispanic community that it once played in the legendary "immigrant Church" of the nineteenth and early twentieth centuries. A Catholic bishop in the Southwest might well apply the resources of his Church to defend the interests of Mexican Catholics on both sides of the border. But the degree to which those Mexicans and/or Mexican Americans would be defended as Catholics as such seems very much open to debate.

The situation is entirely different, however, when we consider not the general Catholic population of the United States, but rather the Catholic priests, nuns, and religious brothers who belong to straightforwardly transnational religious communities that occasion equally straightforwardly transnational identities. In fact, if there ever was a place where American Catholics could be credibly accused (if that is the right word) of holding a religious identity that is in tension with their citizenship, it would be in the seminaries, convents, and other residences of these Catholic orders and communities. One Benedictine monk in Vermont went so far as to tell me that he thought that placing his US citizenship over and above his identification as a Catholic or a Benedictine would be tantamount to blasphemy. That was an unusually emphatic way of putting it, but the general sentiment he was expressing is commonly held among the members of these religious communities.

Nowhere was that sentiment more clearly defined or more politically portentous, however, than among the Maryknoll sisters I talked with in preparing chapter 3 of this book. These women have taken the very unusual step of spending their lives outside their home country as Catholic missionaries, and they become very closely identified with the populations they serve. Their identification with and devotion for the people of Nicaragua, for example, led them to make intense efforts to reverse US foreign policies towards that country that the Maryknoll sisters thought misguided and harmful. These women were fully assimilated into American society: They had been born in the United States and in most cases had been raised in typical American Catholic families. But their distance from American society, in both physical and spiritual terms, was what led them to identify so clearly with the people they lived with and to work so hard to protect the interests of "their people" (of Nicaragua) from the policies of their government (the United States). The Maryknollers occupy a unique space between US citizenship and religious identity, and they explicitly and consciously exploit that position to establish a political role for themselves as informed commentators on the effects that US policy in Central America was actually having on Central Americans.

Finally, ethnic effectiveness is determined by "the degree of homogeneity of a group."[28] Articulation of ethnic identity is facilitated by the degree to which that identity is clearly and exclusively defined. Jews, for example, have an advantage in this regard over Arabs when it comes to pressuring the US government to take sides in disputes in the Middle East. Despite the great diversity of the American Jewish population, it is nevertheless the case that most Jews in the United States identify themselves as Jews rather than as members of another specific national grouping based on geographical origin. This fact has a complex historical basis, of course, and it is an important sign of the degree to which the self-designation "Jewish" is, for many Americans, at least as ethnic in character as it is religious. But the relevant point here is that this broader, less geographically based identity grants an advantage to Jewish lobby groups as they do battle in American pluralist politics with organized Arab interests that are just as likely to be identified as Lebanese or Egyptian or Palestinian as they are to be termed "Arab."

US Catholics are also a diverse population in terms of geographic origin; and that diversity, as I indicate above, militates against the organization of Catholic interests in the context of US foreign policy. But the exact opposite is true when it comes to the men and women who have taken solemn vows as members of specific Catholic religious communities. These men and women share powerful bonds of identity that can easily compete with or even supersede national citizenship. Jesuits have a powerful communal ethos that motivated the entire community when six of its members were murdered. Maryknoll missioners are similarly marked by membership in their community and in particular by their service in mission. And the Benedictine monks of the Weston Priory in Vermont are a particularly tight-knit group of men, defined by their powerful commitment to each other and to the broader Benedictine Confederation. There are only twelve of them at the moment, and although there is a diversity among them in terms of age and background and even national origin, they all share the overwhelmingly powerful cohesiveness of their commitment to a small, stable religious brotherhood. Their political activities—and the brothers are surprisingly political in many ways—are undertaken as a group, in the community's name, without any of the ambiguity or diffuseness that might be associated with the efforts of a larger population.

Even more important, virtually all of the brothers' political activities are undertaken in support of—or as they would rather say, in solidarity with—the work of their Benedictine sisters in Mexico City. This small group of monks in rural Vermont decided long ago to enter into a "covenant relationship" or *alianza* with a group of sisters in Mexico, and that relationship is defined and articulated in the very special vocabulary and values of the Rule of Saint Benedict. Ahrari spoke of the significance of homogeneity in creating the conditions for successful lobbying; perhaps in this case the appropriate word would be "cohesiveness" instead. But whatever we call it, these American men and Mexican women work closely together to disseminate information about what they define as the reality of Mexico. And though any influence they may exert on policy would be indirect and focused on long-term reform, there is no questioning their commitment to changing US foreign policy, or their conviction that it one day will be changed.

Transnational Religion

To return to a crucial point I made earlier, the key to this homogeneity and cohesiveness is the *transnational* nature of these religious communities: the simple but powerful fact that the religious identity shared by members of these communities straddles—and sometimes obliterates—international borders. The point is not that the members of these orders stop being Americans or US citizens. Rather, it is precisely because the Jesuits, Maryknollers, and Benedictines are both US citizens and members of transnational religious communities that they are able to bring their communities' interests to the policymaking processes in the United States with such legitimacy.[29] They are, in a sense, insiders to both realms, and that special status provides them with both (a) the motivation to care deeply about US foreign policy and (b) the opportunity to try to influence its direction.

When Robert Keohane and Joseph Nye first identified "transnational interactions" as a category of international relations, they were in a sense identifying a space or an arena of interaction as much as they were defining a type of behavior or interaction. Their original identification of "the movement of tangible or intangible items across state boundaries when at least one actor is not an agent of a government or an intergovernmental organization" was from the beginning closely related to the literature on global civil society and all of its many variants focused on nonstate actors in world politics.[30] The idea was that not all relevant interactions across internationally recognized borders involve relations between two states, or even between states and intergovernmental institutions. Instead, a wide variety of actors—from multinational corporations to epistemic communities to global organized interests to, yes, transnational religious communities—are also interacting in a global space that is not exclusively defined by territorially sovereign states and that has qualities in common with the free, nongovernmentally controlled domestic space that social scientists define as civil society.

In the ensuing years other scholars have followed Keohane and Nye's lead in drawing attention to this category of actor and transaction, and some of them have usefully shifted their focus to the specific forms of transnational contestation or contention that take place within these expanded spaces of global politics. In their groundbreaking work *Activists beyond Borders*, for example, Margaret Keck and Kathryn Sikkink identify a phenomenon they call the "boomerang effect." According to this dynamic, "domestic NGOs [nongovernmental organizations] bypass their states and directly search out international allies to try to bring pressure on their states from outside."[31] This kind of transnational politics requires deep connections between activists inside the target state and influential actors outside of it, and it is just the kind of connection and pathway that I examine here in *Reverse Mission*.

The Jesuit priests in El Salvador, for example, were not an NGO in the traditional sense of that term. But when they sought to bring pressure on the Salvadoran government in response to the murder of six of their members, they did so in part by working in close coordination with their fellow Jesuits in the United States. Their Jesuit brothers in the United States shared their outrage over the atrocities taking place in El Salvador, but the American Jesuits also had a level of access to the foreign policymaking process in Washington that the Jesuits in El Salvador could never hope to gain on their own. Keck and Sikkink call this "searching out international allies"; the Jesuits themselves would probably prefer to describe it as relying on the support of their brothers.[32] But the effect is the same: a boomerang of transnational advocacy on the basis of shared identity and shared interests within a religious community that has members both in El Salvador and in the United States of America.

Throwing an even wider net, Sidney Tarrow developed a category of actors he called "rooted cosmopolitans," defined as "individuals and groups who mobilize domestic and international resources and opportunities to advance claims on behalf of external actors, against external opponents, or in favor of goals they hold in common with transnational allies."[33] It is hard to imagine any group of people more rooted than the community of brothers who have decided to spend their lives in a small Benedictine monastery on a Vermont mountainside. But to a degree that frankly surprised me as I got to know this community over a number of years of observation, the brothers of the Weston Priory are also quite outward-looking in their outlook and in their commitments. I would say, in fact, that they conform quite closely to that subset of actors that Tarrow called "transnational activists." The Benedictine brothers, in other words, are "people . . . who are rooted in specific national contexts [I'll say!], but who engage in contentious political activities that involve them in transnational networks of contacts and conflicts." The *alianza* with their sisters in Mexico is the motivation and the glue that leads these men to "draw on the resources, networks, and opportunities of the societies they live in" in an effort to reform US policies that they see as harmful to their Mexican sisters and to the Mexican society in which those sisters live and work.[34]

Tarrow himself cited missionaries as early practitioners of this kind of transnational contention.[35] I certainly saw these dynamics at work in the Maryknoll community in the context of its work in Nicaragua. The Maryknoll missioners developed a very powerful shared identity with the people with whom they lived and worked in Nicaragua. But when it came time to take political action to protect those people from the effects of US foreign policy in the region, the Maryknoll women returned home to the United States for the purpose of evangelizing their fellow US citizens. In part, this focus was a function of the overwhelming effects that US policy can have on the peoples of Central America. But the missioners also engaged in reverse mission because despite all the years they had spent out of the country, and despite all the solidarity they felt for the people of Nicaragua, these women remained US citizens. Therefore, it was through a return to their roots in the United States that these women were best able to mobilize the resources at their disposal "in favor of goals they [held] in common with transnational allies."[36]

Looking at the Jesuit priests, Maryknoll missioners, and Benedictine monks in this way raises the possibility that the members of these particular religious communities might be doubly rooted in politically significant ways.[37] Yes, the citizenship that almost all of these men and women hold in the United States affords them an insider status and an access to American policymaking processes that their brothers and sisters abroad are systematically denied. But the cosmopolitanism of these citizens is limited by the degree to which their religious formation and life experience have also rooted them in the religious communities that have played such a central part in defining their individual and collective identities. In a complex sense that returns us to Ahrari's categorization of ethnic mobilization outlined earlier, these priests, nuns, and monks, in advocating for their brothers and sisters abroad, were acting out of permanent, virtually familial commitments that rooted them both in their religious communities and in the national policy processes that affected those communities so profoundly.

The political dynamics that I am interested in exploring here are profoundly shaped by the specific nature of those policymaking processes in the United States. Like ethnic lobbying groups, the political role of transnational religious communities is shaped by specific intersections between the nature of the religious communities themselves and the nature of the processes of making US foreign policy. As we will see in the case studies, these processes offer advantages to some religious interests in some contexts, and they offer disadvantages to others in other contexts. As Thomas Risse-Kappen argued many years ago, domestic political structures powerfully mediate the influence of all transnational actors in contemporary international relations.[38] It is not enough to focus on the nature of the individual transnational actor, or even on the specific nature of the actor's political activities. We also have to recognize that these specific transnational actors are embedded in equally specific domestic political structures and political processes that shape the sort of influence they can have on public policy.

That is certainly the case in terms of the three transnational religious communities I study in this book. A number of years ago Susanne Rudolph and James Piscatori edited a book titled *Transnational Religion and Fading States*.[39] It is a fine book, and it is a valuable contribution to the literature I rely on here. But in my judgment the title is an unfortunate overstatement. States are not "fading"—not in terms of their relationship with transnational religion, anyway. On the contrary, sovereign states serve still as the central arenas in which transnational religions assert themselves; and individual states still constitute the central set of structures that transnational religions seek to direct and influence. To be sure, there is now a complex entity called global civil society, and transnational Catholic religious communities do indeed reside within it, in a manner of speaking. But what members of these communities do most of the time, in terms of political activity, is rely on the relationships they enjoy beyond the boundaries of a single sovereign state as the foundation for their attempts to influence the policies of individual states. These religious communities are engaged in *transnational* contentious action. But the target of that action—in the cases I examine here—is quite *national* in nature; it is simply the government and foreign policy of the United States of America. Or perhaps a bit less grandly in the case of the Benedictines, the target is the awareness, attitudes, and long-term commitments of US citizens.

The fact that these communities carry out these political activities in such distinctive ways, and in ways so closely related to their own religious missions and commitments, is what makes them so interesting to me analytically and so emblematic of a much wider phenomenon. These Jesuits, Maryknollers, and Benedictines act politically out of a powerful sense of shared identity and solidarity with their brothers and sisters abroad. But in each and every case, they act as Jesuits, as Maryknollers, and as Benedictines, through styles and approaches that are all their own and that are fully consonant with the self-conception of their communities. Jesuit university professors, for example, undergo the processes of discernment called for by their Spiritual Exercises, express themselves as members of a transnational society, and seek to use their institutional clout to bring about political change to ease the suffering of the men they call "ours." Maryknoll missioners are just that, missioners. So when they are inspired and driven to act in defense of the interests of the people they are accompanying in other countries, they do what they know best how to do. They evangelize; they seek to convert their fellow American citizens to the cause of justice and peace abroad.

And Benedictine monks in Vermont? They likewise do what Benedictines always do and have done for 1,500 years: They root themselves in the stability of a particular local community. But they also dedicate themselves with signal fervor to the Benedictine practice of hospitality; they leave themselves open to the experiences of others, particularly of their sisters in Mexico, by figuratively and literally leaving open the doors of their monastic home.

In all three cases these Catholic men and women formulate their personal and communal identities in large measure out of their participation in transnational brotherhood and sisterhood. They are citizens of the United States, but they are also members of a much broader and deeply felt collectivity—and those two identities can sometimes clash with one another. In the pages that follow I leave largely for others to answer the normative questions of whether such complex identities are appropriate, or whether such competing loyalties are problematic. I am much more interested in the analytical questions of how those loyalties are developed, how they get turned into political activism, and how they differ across a series of apparently similar cases. Careful attention to such analysis will enhance understanding of a relatively unexamined corner of religious politics in contemporary America, populated by priests and nuns with deep and sharply articulated interests in US foreign policy. But such attention will also awaken us, in a more general sense, to the ways in which identities are contingent, loyalties are complex, and political mobilizations arise out of relationships and intersections that our all-too-common singular focus on national citizenship and on state-level politics makes it all too easy to miss.

CHAPTER 2

Ours

Martyrdom in El Salvador, Mobilization in the United States

The rose garden outside the Pastoral Center at the Universidad Centroamericana José Simeón Cañas (UCA) in San Salvador is now a site of pilgrimage, a place where countless visitors come to sit, reflect, and usually pray. This placid spot along the back edge of the university used to be just the yard behind a house where several of the Jesuit priests who served as administrators and faculty lived. But the beautiful, lush garden was planted in grief and homage by Obdulio Ramos after his wife, Elba, her daughter Celina, and six of the Jesuit priests were murdered at the site on November 16, 1989. The sad irony is that Elba Ramos, who served as a cook for the priests, had stayed with the Jesuits on that fateful night because she thought that she and her daughter would be safer there than in their own nearby home. The Farabundo Martí National Liberation Front (FMLN), who had been fighting the Salvadoran government for years in a seemingly endless civil war, had launched an offensive inside the capital city, and the neighborhood surrounding the UCA was engulfed in urban warfare. Elba and Celina Ramos chose to stay with the Jesuits that night because they assumed that neither the guerillas nor the army would have the audacity to attack or harm the priests.

They assumed wrong. The Salvadoran Army had audacity to spare. Under the cover of the guerilla offensive, and with the futile hope that the atrocity could be blamed later on opposition forces, soldiers from the Atlacatl Battalion of the Salvadoran Army roused five of the priests from their sleep, forced them out into the yard where the rose garden now blooms, laid them side by side on their stomachs, and then methodically shot each of them with a single bullet in the back of the head. Wishing to ensure that there would be no witnesses to the crime, the soldiers then searched the Jesuits' residence, where they found one more priest as well as Elba Ramos and her daughter. The priest was killed and dragged back into his room. The cook and her daughter were shot to death in a hail of bullets as they clung to each other in a guest bedroom in the house.[1]

The Salvadoran Army not only had audacity to spare, they also had stupidity to match. It is hard to imagine that army doing anything more antithetical to their own military and political goals in late 1989 than assassinating the Jesuit leadership of the UCA. For in killing Ignacio Ellacuría, Segundo Montes, Ignacio Martín-Baró, Armondo López, Juan Ramón Moreno, and Joaquín López y López, the Salvadoran Army succeeded in drawing tremendous attention to the one group of people in all of El Salvador who probably had the closest, deepest, and longest relationship with politically significant people in the United States of any group in the country. In retrospect it is fair to say that if the leadership of the Salvadoran Army had actually wanted to excite opposition to its goals within the United States—if the Salvadoran generals had actually wanted to encourage calls to cut off US military aid to El Salvador and embolden those within the United States who supported a negotiated political settlement in El Salvador—then they could probably not have taken a more effective action than to murder Jesuit priests in cold blood on the back lawn of the UCA.

The Salvadoran priests were members of a transnational brotherhood of twenty thousand members called the Society of Jesus. That society included in 1989 about four thousand members who were citizens of the United States of America, the majority of whom were college and university professors. Some of these American citizens knew the Salvadoran martyrs personally. Many more of them knew the Salvadorans by reputation as men who were trying to breathe new life into the Jesuits' educational apostolate, or mission activity, and to infuse their university in El Salvador with the

Jesuit mission of "the service of faith and the promotion of justice."[2] But nearly all of the United States–based Jesuits were outraged to learn that six of their brothers, six of "ours," had been assassinated by a military force that was supported, funded, and directed by their own US government. And because they were Jesuits, formed by a religious community that prizes turning discernment into action, Jesuit priests in the United States were anxious to transform their instinctive outrage into concerted political action.

Ours

The murders at the UCA meant many things, but the most practical ramification was that a university in El Salvador had now been robbed of its leadership. Decisions needed to be made; funds needed to be raised; classes needed to be taught. To put it most prosaically, staff needed to be replaced. In a secular university in the United States, such a crisis of leadership would be met with interim appointments, internal promotions, and expedited search processes. But for the Society of Jesus, a transnational brotherhood at its core, the natural response was to form a replacement team outside of the country and send that team immediately to El Salvador.

Charles Beirne, a Jesuit priest known by everyone as Charlie before he died in 2010, was in 1989 the academic vice president of Santa Clara University in California's Silicon Valley. He had a lot of experience working in Central America, and he knew Ellacuría and the other murdered priests well.[3] He had been calling the Jesuits at the UCA each night since the guerilla offensive had been launched, assuring himself and the Jesuit community at Santa Clara that their friends in El Salvador were safe. As a matter of fact, Beirne's first reaction on hearing that something terrible had happened at the UCA was to think that there must be some mistake, since he had spoken with Martín-Baró just the evening before. Beirne was helping Martín-Baró publish an article about conditions in El Salvador under an assumed name, and on the night of November 15, Beirne had been assured that, although military forces had searched the Jesuit residence and surrounded the university, all of the residents of the house were accounted for and safe. That safety was brutally violated later that night, of course. When Beirne was informed by officials at the Jesuit Conference later that morning that the six had been murdered, his second reaction, after a first wave of shock and grief, was to realize that his life "was changed forever."[4]

Dean Brackley, another Jesuit, was in the fall of 1989 just starting to teach theology at Fordham University in New York City.[5] Brackley did not fit the usual mold of Jesuit academic, in either affect or background. He had spent years doing pastoral work among the poor in the Bronx, and like many of his fellow Jesuits he wondered whether the Society of Jesus was overinvested in American higher education. He did not know the Salvadorans personally, but when he heard the news that morning in November, he too had a very personal reaction. Any Jesuit sent to carry on the work of the UCA, he wrote later, "would have to know Spanish and be able to do university work. He would have to be familiar with the situation in Central America and have had some experience working among the poor. Hmmm," he thought, "how many of us could there be?"[6]

As it turns out, many Jesuits, both in the United States and throughout the world, reacted the same way that Beirne and Brackley did. They mourned the loss of their fellow Jesuits—and they volunteered to replace them. In a sense, the Jesuits who had been murdered at the UCA embodied the transnational structure of the Society of Jesus. Most had spent their entire adult lives working and teaching in El Salvador, but they were themselves Spaniards, not native Salvadorans. Indeed, the fact that they were not native-born citizens had been used in propaganda against the UCA. The Jesuits, according to the Salvadoran government, were not conscientious Salvadorans expressing concern for their fellow citizens; they were illegitimate foreigners serving as outside agitators in support of an international communist conspiracy.[7]

In any event, the decision of whom to assign to the replacement team at the UCA fell to Peter Kolvenbach, the then superior general of the Society of Jesus. "The General," as superiors general are universally known among Jesuits, sits atop a remarkably hierarchical authority structure that governs Jesuits throughout the world. Headquartered in Rome, the superior general is advised and supported by a number of assistants, each of whom is responsible for a specified geographic area, known as an assistancy. There is an assistant for Central America and Mexico, for example, and another for the United States. The assistants, however, serve as a more or less administrative level of support for the general in his governance of the Society. The actual religious authority lines run directly from the superior general to the ninety-three provincials who govern the various Jesuit provinces around the globe. Central America makes up a single province, whereas there are ten provinces spread out across the United States. Each Jesuit takes a vow of obedience, and that obedience is owed, as a practical matter, to the provincial as a direct representative of the superior general, also called the father general, in Rome. The military structure and nomenclature is no accident. The Society of Jesus, after all, was founded in the sixteenth century by Saint Ignatius of Loyola, a military nobleman from the Basque region of Spain.[8]

There are literally hundreds of Catholic orders of priests and nuns around the world; and as we will see throughout this book, each of these orders, or communities, has its own history, tradition, ethos, and charism (or gift of grace). Some, like the Benedictines, are monastic or contemplative orders. Members of these orders live out a commitment to stability, that is, to a decision to root themselves in one place and one community for a lifetime of prayer, work, and often silence. Others, like the Maryknoll community, are missionary orders, and their commitment is to uproot themselves utterly to spend a lifetime bringing either Christian conversion to pagans, according to the traditional mission, or companionship to the poor, according to today's emerging notion of modern missionary work. Jesuits, however, are neither monastic nor missionary—they are something, in a sense, in between. Sometimes called "contemplatives in action," members of the Society of Jesus ideally are committed through their vows of obedience to mobility and to a process of spiritual discernment that will lead to an active engagement with the world that is focused above all on the notion of bringing all things to God.

Saint Ignatius was a man of the Counter-Reformation, and his intention was to found a community of men (unlike many other Catholic orders, the Society of Jesus is still exclusively male) who would offer their services freely to the papacy. Jesuits would be entirely free of connections to particular places; be open to mobility, both physically and spiritually; be committed only to the transnational community as a whole; and be profoundly available to be sent by the pope wherever he felt they could be of the greatest use to him and to the Church. Ignatius himself was deeply attached to this value of mobility, and he is reported to have chafed against the stable residence in Rome that was imposed on him late in his life by his duties as the Society's first superior general.

Today, mobility for many Jesuits has been replaced by tenured professorships in colleges and universities. The lives of many Jesuits in the United States today are characterized by a comfortable stability that would rival the stationary existence of any monastic monk: more contemplation than action. One former provincial humorously defined the commitment to mobility by many modern Jesuits as "an unshakable commitment to move anywhere the provincial asks him to. . . . anywhere, that is, on the island of Manhattan."[9] The fact that the principle is respected as much in the breach as in the practice, however, does not mean that the principle itself does not exist. Mobility remains part of the Jesuit ethos, and it manifests itself communally, if not always individually, in pervasive ways throughout the order. In the most basic sense Jesuits tend to be travelers. Their seminaries can be veritable Towers of Babel, occupied by Jesuits from all over the world studying philosophy or theology or engaging in the pastoral or educational work of what they call their regency. I have often been surprised that Jesuits of my acquaintance do not know each other—provincial walls can sometimes be high—but I am never surprised to meet in the dining room of a Jesuit residence visitors from all over the world, whether they are studying or working in a given location or just passing through. Sometimes I have pictured the Society of Jesus as a kind of global network of hostels, where traveling Jesuits show up spontaneously at doors all over the world and are welcomed spontaneously and unquestioningly as "one of ours."

Men like Charlie Beirne and Dean Brackley, then, were self-consciously reaffirming the traditional Jesuit principle of mobility when they offered to drop their work in the United States and move to El Salvador to help run the UCA. But they were also acting out of a process that all Jesuits call discernment: the idea that prayer and reflection can lead to imperfect knowledge of God's will, and that once that knowledge is gained, discernment must lead to *action*. In describing his own haste to accept the challenges and dangers of working at the UCA, Beirne later stressed that "there is so much in Jesuit spirituality of discernment, and of looking at the reality. You cannot stay with contemplation, though," he added, "you have to act. You have to turn it all into action."[10]

Making a similar point, Brackley relied on somewhat more homey imagery in describing his personal process of discernment. "An image floated spontaneously to mind," he wrote, "a fastball coming across the middle of the plate. . . . I couldn't tell from the way I felt whether God was inviting me to swing at this pitch or not. But neither did any solid reasons arise for not swinging." I have read more eloquent accounts of the discernment process, but Brackley's description sums up well the relationship between discernment and obedience in the Jesuit ethos. "Life is short," he concluded. "Besides, the odds were good that if I offered to go they would turn me down!"[11]

Over the course of working on this project, I asked every single Jesuit I met (and there have been dozens) what it is that holds the Society together as a community. These men have differed enormously in every way: different ages, nationalities, temperaments, political persuasions, professional backgrounds. But every single one of them gave me exactly the same answer spontaneously—the Spiritual Exercises of Saint Ignatius of Loyola. The Spiritual Exercises, also known as "the long retreat," constitute a thirty-day experience that every Jesuit has gone through since Ignatius began directing his earlier followers almost five hundred years ago. Once during the novitiate (just before taking vows and formally entering the Society), and once again about twenty or so years later as a kind of refresher course, each Jesuit spends four weeks in a period of prayer and reflection meant to heighten his awareness of God in his life and to deepen his understanding of the ways in which he, as a human being and a member of the Society of Jesus, should discern the best way in which he can act to bring all things to God.

Jesuits have described it to me as a "shared mystical experience," a "mystical tie," a "way of proceeding," and a "very particular way of understanding the Gospels." Here is not the place for a detailed description of the Exercises themselves.[12] For my purposes it is sufficient to say that the experience has two relevant effects on the Jesuit community and its transnational structure and worldview. The first is that the Spiritual Exercises train each Jesuit throughout the world to approach spirituality and the religious life in a remarkably consistent way. Charlie Beirne's talk of discernment and his conviction that contemplation must lead to action could come out of the mouth of virtually every Jesuit in the world. They wear that understanding of the relationship between prayer and action, faith and justice, as a common cloak that defines their life's work and their shared identity. The second effect of the Exercises is that no matter what the content of the experience, the fact that all Jesuits cite the Exercises as the glue of their communal life is a remarkably powerful shared experience in and of itself. I would argue that the very universality of the answer they gave to my question is itself a form of solidarity that has powerfully unifying effects. I mean in no way to denigrate its real effects. But as a symbol of unity, as a vehicle of rootedness in the Society, as a kind of secret handshake shared by twenty thousand men all over the world, the Spiritual Exercises are a powerful force indeed.

So with mobility in mind, and after efforts at the kind of discernment called for by the Spiritual Exercises, dozens of Jesuits from around the world volunteered their services to the UCA in the days immediately following the murders in November 1989. Charlie Beirne was able to offer himself directly to Father General Kolvenbach, who happened to be visiting Santa Clara University on other business just weeks after the murders. Dean Brackley, on the other hand, worked through his provincial in New York City. In both cases, however, their offers were accepted, and within a matter of a very few months these two Americans from the New York Province of Jesuits joined Michael Czerny of Canada, Rafael De Sivette and Juan Lecuona of Spain, and Fernando Azuela of Mexico in picking up the work at the UCA in San Salvador. The broadly international character of the replacement team is emblematic of Jesuit practice.

But for my purposes the most interesting thing is the fact that two members of the chosen team were citizens of the United States. What did that mean to the Salvadoran Jesuits who at that time wondered whether they would be next—whether the Salvadoran right would make good on an old and never-rescinded threat to kill every Jesuit priest in the country? And what did it mean to Beirne and Brackley as American citizens to be placed in such a politically complex position? They were Jesuits; that was perhaps the fundamental content of their personal identity, and that was what had brought them to El Salvador. But they were also North Americans, *gringos*, citizens of the United States, the same United States that was sending $1.5 million a day to the army that had just murdered their brothers.

Charlie Beirne, though clearly the more political of the two in terms of personal outlook, tended in interviews to define his response and availability in terms of friendship and solidarity. "Some of it was the bonds of friendship," he recalled. "I knew all the guys who were killed; I knew the Central American provincial."[13] Beirne had met Ellacuría at a Jesuit meeting in Lima, Peru, many years before and had seen him at other international meetings and in El Salvador over the ensuing years. He had visited their community in El Salvador and felt that in taking up Martín-Baró's post as the UCA's academic vice president he was, as much as anything else, engaging in an act of personal Jesuit brotherhood. Dean Brackley did not know the murdered Jesuits personally, though he shared the powerful sense of solidarity that drew both him and Beirne to the UCA. But while describing himself as "on the fringes" of the political firestorm that surrounded the UCA in those days, Brackley nevertheless defined his own discernment and decision in decidedly political terms. "There is no question," he told me, "that I came [to El Salvador] as an act of civic responsibility or even patriotism, paying my dues as an American citizen or paying reparations, you might say."[14]

This was not the dual citizenship of a Catholic American who could not be trusted because of his fealty to a foreign potentate, that is, the "Pope of Rome." This was a US citizen who felt responsible for what *his* government was doing to *his* brothers. This was another form of dual loyalty: not one that competed with American citizenship, but rather one that challenged these American citizens to do all they could, as American citizens, to bring about change in policies that were harmful, in this case murderously so, to their religious brothers abroad. And this challenge and the responsibilities that came with it were felt in the American Jesuit community well beyond the two men, Charlie Beirne and Dean Brackley, who through their Jesuit commitments to mobility and discernment made themselves available to take the place of the fallen martyrs in El Salvador.

Jesuit Universities

That responsibility may have been felt most acutely by the men who served as presidents of Jesuit colleges and universities in the United States. The six dead men in San Salvador were fellow Jesuits, yes. But Ignacio Ellacuría was even more than that; he was a fellow president (or *rector*, in Salvadoran parlance) of a Jesuit institution of higher learning. In the words of the late Paul Locatelli, the Jesuit former president of Santa Clara University in California, "we knew what they [the Salvadoran military] were trying to do."[15] They were trying to silence the voice of Jesuit education in Salvadoran society. So that voice would be revived and echoed by the spokesmen for Jesuit education in the United States.

Leo O'Donovan, who was then the Jesuit president of Georgetown University in Washington, DC, remembered that he cried that morning because of the deeply personal intensity of his identification with Ellacuría and his colleagues.[16] Donald Monan, the Jesuit former president of Boston College, used the word "horrified" to describe his reaction, a reaction that led him to a deep personal involvement in what came to be called "the Jesuit case" in El Salvador.[17] For example, this rather courtly leader of a major university in a major American city sat in the courtroom in El Salvador two years later as the verdicts were read in the trial of the military officers charged with plotting and carrying out the murders at the UCA.

All of these men sprang into action in the days immediately following the murders, applying the resources of their prominent institutions to bring attention to the outrage that had been perpetrated with "bullets made in the U.S.A.," as one Jesuit put it.[18] O'Donovan, leader of what he called "the most powerful university in Washington," was particularly well positioned to play a public role.[19] He published an op-ed piece in the *Washington Post* on November 19, 1989, just three days after the killings, calling the UCA one of Georgetown's "sister schools" and referring to the Salvadoran Jesuits as his "brothers." Citing the "urgent need" for an immediate cease-fire, as Ellacuría had been doing for years, O'Donovan also called for aggressive investigation of a crime that even in those early days most Jesuits in both El Salvador and the United States believed had been carried out by the Salvadoran army.[20]

In addition, in a kind of coincidence that demonstrated both the importance of Jesuit education and the transnational reach of the Jesuit community, O'Donovan was also able to meet personally with Salvadoran president Alfredo Christiani because Christiani was himself a graduate of Georgetown University. "I am not a firebrand," O'Donovan told me in an interview, "and not much for demonstrativeness. But I was horrified and I told [Christiani] that I didn't know the facts, but you have to find them, and the extent to which you don't you are going to lose support in the US."[21]

Joseph O'Hare, who was at the time of the murders the Jesuit president of Fordham University, told me that there was at the time a "special kinship between people who were struggling with the whole idea of what is the mission of a Catholic university and, in fact, a Jesuit university that had the mandate of faith and justice."[22] Given this shared challenge or commitment, and also surely because he was the most prominent Jesuit priest in New York City, O'Hare was tapped by the New York provincial to give the main homily at a mass that was held that first week at Saint Ignatius Loyola Jesuit Church on Park Avenue in Manhattan. Referring explicitly to these institutional connections, O'Hare stated that "for the Jesuits working at the twenty-eight Jesuit colleges and universities in [the United States], there is an added sense of solidarity with the martyrs." But then, turning that identification into a call for political action, O'Hare also said that "after ten years of evasions and equivocation . . . the assassinations of November 16 pose, with brutal clarity, the question that continues to haunt the policy of the United

States towards El Salvador: Can we hand weapons to butchers and remain unstained by the blood of their innocent victims?"[23]

O'Hare captured as well as anyone else the dual theme of Jesuit reaction in the United States in those early days, with his expression of solidarity with the fallen Jesuits along with his conviction that their brutal murders had uncovered a fundamental truth about the brutality of US policy in El Salvador. That same dual message was delivered by Jesuits across the United States, but not only by individuals. The cause was also immediately taken up by the Association of Jesuit Colleges and Universities (AJCU), an organization that seeks to coordinate the missions and activities of the presidents and administrations of schools like Georgetown, Fordham, and Boston College, as well as others like the University of San Francisco, Marquette University, and Loyola University of Baltimore.[24] The first response of the AJCU—led at the time by Paul Tipton, an energetic force with an eye for politics—was to send five of its university presidents to El Salvador in February 1990 to serve as a tangible sign of the interest that the US Jesuits had both in the Jesuit case itself and in the wider question of American policy in Central America.

The five presidents—a group that included, by the way, both O'Hare of Fordham and Monan of Boston College—met during their stay with every notable on the Salvadoran scene, from President Christiani and his top military officers to Ambassador William Walker at the US embassy. Monan recalls now that the trip had one very practical ramification. "At the time the Jesuits weren't sure whether this was an isolated incident against this group of people," he told me in an interview," or whether it was going to be directed against the Society [of Jesus] itself."[25] In the context of real physical danger for the Salvadoran Jesuits, in other words, expressions of solidarity by men like Monan and O'Hare were not simply pleasant sentiment. They were a form of North American protection for men who went to bed each night not knowing whether they would be roused and murdered before morning.[26]

At the same time, however, the trip also was a step toward trying to answer the challenging question that O'Hare had asked in his sermon in New York. How could the United States support a government, these Jesuits asked, that seemed patently unwilling to launch a true investigation that might produce not only the enlisted men who pulled the triggers on the Jesuits but, much more importantly, the "intellectual authors" of the crime?[27] "We went down there and saw everybody," O'Hare recalled. "It was an ominous atmosphere. . . . The US embassy was like an armed camp. . . . In retrospect, we felt like they gave us a bunch of baloney and whitewash."[28] As Monan described it, "We wanted to use our presence as presidents of US Jesuit universities to put some pressure on the [Salvadoran] government to really get at the truth." But as the Jesuits would learn only too well in the coming months and years, such a desire was pretty much doomed to result in frustration. "Christiani was polite," Monan recalled. "They were all seemingly cooperative. But we hit the same stone wall that the Jesuits in El Salvador had hit."[29]

That stone wall was receiving a great deal of attention at the time. The Jesuits were not the only ones upset at the events in San Salvador, or at the apparent unwillingness of the Salvadoran government to give up the crime's intellectual authors, or at the equally apparent unwillingness of the US embassy to pressure the Salvadoran government to do so. The CBS News television show *60 Minutes* produced a segment on the murders and their aftermath, emphasizing both the reluctant nature of the Salvadoran investigation and the acquiescence of the US embassy. President O'Hare of Fordham University and President Monan of Boston College were both featured in that report. O'Hare spoke for many when he pointed out on *60 Minutes* that the murders at the UCA were only the latest in a series of atrocities that had been committed in El Salvador, atrocities that had been either ignored or swept under the rug by the Salvadoran government and by that government's American paymasters. Once again, because their brothers in El Salvador had been particular targets of some of those earlier atrocities, Jesuits in the United States were particularly outraged that the atrocities had apparently been committed with impunity.

Be a Patriot, Kill a Priest

The name Rutilio Grande is hardly a household name in the United States of America. But mention his name in any of the Jesuit households across the country, and everyone there is sure to be aware of him. Grande was a Jesuit priest who was murdered in 1977 in the Salvadoran town of Aquilares for the "crime" of encouraging landless, penniless peasants to organize in defense of their interests and their rights.[30] Such encouragement was defined as subversive by the Salvadoran government and its paramilitary supporters, and Grande's murder was a very clear signal to Jesuits and other Catholic clergy that religious actors who sought to apply the message of Jesus Christ to the profoundly inequitable political and economic structures of Salvadoran society would be dealt with harshly. Grande's death has been called "a defining event for the Jesuits of Central America, and for the Salvadoran church," but I would extend that judgment to include Jesuits in the United States as well.[31]

The Jesuit community in the United States is a relatively diverse entity. Divided by age, by profession (the chasm between "high school Jesuits" and "college Jesuits" can sometimes be particularly wide), and simply by political ideology, the members of the Society of Jesus did not all have the same reaction at the time to liberation theology or to the appearance of political activism on the part of Jesuits in El Salvador, Nicaragua, and elsewhere in Latin America. But Grande's murder caught the attention of everyone, left and right, on the Jesuit political spectrum. Some worried that Grande and his ilk had wandered across a thin line between pastoral care and political leadership; others wanted the whole institutional Catholic Church to devote its resources and energies to the kind of social mobilization for which Grande had been killed. But no Jesuits in the United States were able to ignore Grande's death. And fewer were able to dismiss it when shortly thereafter the White Warriors Union (a notorious paramilitary death squad in El Salvador) ordered all Jesuits to leave El Salvador within thirty days to avoid meeting the same bloody fate as Rutilio Grande. "Be a Patriot," the accompanying pamphlets and signs read, "kill a priest!"[32]

The Jesuits did not leave El Salvador in thirty days. Nor were they all killed, as the grisly promise was never carried out. Nevertheless, Salvadoran Jesuit resolve and US Jesuit solidarity were both deepened and strengthened by Grande's death and by the White Warriors Union's brazen threat. And even more significant for the visibility of events in El Salvador, and for the degree of attention that small country received in Catholic circles in the United States, Grande's death had a powerful effect on the thinking and life of Oscar Romero, archbishop of San Salvador. Chosen for that crucial post by Pope Paul VI in 1977 because of his reputation for cautious pragmatism, the Salvadoran archbishop was profoundly transformed by the death of his close personal friend Rutilio Grande. Shocked that Grande could be killed for performing pastoral work among simple peasants, Romero underwent a public conversion that played itself out over three dramatic years.[33] Known by some as "Rutilio's miracle," this transformation of a quiet conservative bishop into an outspoken critic of the Salvadoran regime was a major turning point in the development of Salvadoran politics and society.[34] Explicitly identifying himself with the suffering of the poor in El Salvador, Romero dedicated himself and his Church to the task of serving, as he said countless times, as the "voice of the voiceless."[35]

In one of his most dramatic statements, Romero went as far as to declare that "it would be sad, if in a country where murder is being committed so horribly, were we not to find priests also among the victims. They are the testimony of a church incarnated in the problems of its people."[36] As the country got more tense, and as threats against his own life got ever more explicit, Romero's rhetoric got more and more blunt and, from the point of view of the government, more and more incendiary. On Sunday, March 23, 1980, the archbishop ended his weekly sermon (all of which were broadcast to the whole country on Catholic radio) with a direct appeal to the soldiers and officers of the Salvadoran military. "In the name of God," he said to Catholic Salvadorans whom he was accusing of oppressing other Catholic Salvadorans, "and in the name of this suffering people, whose laments rise to heaven each day more tumultuous, I beg you, I beseech you, I order you in the name of God: Stop the repression! Thou shalt not kill! Stop the repression!"[37] The very next day, as he celebrated mass at the chapel of Divine Providence Hospital, next to the small apartment that had been his humble home as archbishop, Oscar Romero was killed with a single bullet to the heart.

In both life and death Romero's relationship with the Society of Jesus had been shrouded in controversy. Some of the faculty at the UCA recalled that they were "anything but enthusiastic" about a "bleak future" under Romero as their archbishop; they were especially appalled at his relationship with the conservative group Opus Dei, and they presumed that he would oppose their theological projects and seek to frustrate the social mission of their university.[38] That presumption was what made "Rutilio's miracle" such a welcome wonder for the Jesuits. And the undeniably surprising nature of Romero's conversion is what led many Salvadorans outside the UCA to accuse the Jesuits of manipulating an archbishop who, these critics charged, was overwhelmed by the complexities of his new responsibilities. Regardless of where one comes down on this question of the relationship between Romero and the Jesuits in the last years of his life, there is no doubt that the Jesuits joined wholeheartedly in the lionization of the archbishop after his death. They participated prominently in Romero's funeral (an event, by the way, fired upon by the ever more brazen Salvadoran military); they opened a pastoral center in Romero's name at the UCA (which the army later burned and ransacked on the night of the murders in November 1989); and they defined their work from that point on as carrying on the mission of their martyred leader. Ellacuría himself phrased most plainly, and even hyperbolically, the Jesuits' view of Romero, when he said at a memorial service at the UCA in late March 1980: "With Archbishop Romero, God has visited El Salvador."[39]

What is most significant for my purposes here, however, and for the role that Romero played in strengthening the transnational Jesuit ties between El Salvador and the United States, is that the Jesuits at the UCA conceived of themselves as furthering Romero's mission not only as priests but *universidadamente*, as a university.[40] That particular emphasis is very important because these events were taking place in El Salvador at the same time that a debate was being conducted within Jesuit circles throughout the world over the proper role and mission of Jesuit universities. To put the matter in terms specific to the United States, places like Georgetown University and Boston College had succeeded in becoming major centers of higher

learning in one of the richest, most technologically advanced societies in the world. Competing with the major secular universities of
the Ivy League and elsewhere, these Jesuit institutions had "arrived"
institutionally. Not incidentally they had also served as vehicles of
social mobility for American Catholics, both in fact and in percep-
tion. But what now, many were asking? What about these universities was still grounded in Jesuit principles or a Jesuit mission? What
distinguished them as Jesuit institutions, in comparison to secular
American universities?

These were controversial questions among the Jesuit community in the United States, not least because they really were hard
questions to answer. But Ignacio Ellacuría and his colleagues at the
UCA were providing an answer. It was a challenging answer for US
Jesuits to accept, but it was an answer nevertheless, and it was a
fairly simple one. According to Ellacuría Jesuits ought to devote the
energy and resources of their universities to uncover the inequali-
ties and injustices of the societies in which they were housed *and* to
propose solutions that would make those societies more equitable,
more just, and more open to the liberating message of the Gospel
of Jesus Christ. In a vocabulary drawn directly out of Jesuit mission
statements, the leaders of the Universidad Centroamericana were
arguing that Jesuit universities throughout the world ought to be
structured and run in "the service of faith and the promotion of
justice."

Service of Faith, Promotion of Justice

The Society of Jesus, as much as any other transnational community of priests and nuns, was deeply affected by the tumult that engulfed the Roman Catholic Church in the 1960s. In 1965, the year
when the Second Vatican Council closed in Rome, the Jesuits chose
as their new father general a man named Pedro Arrupe. Only the
second Basque to lead the Society since Ignatius of Loyola himself,
Arrupe was, in the words of one observer, "dedicated to the renewal
of the Society of Jesus' commitment to justice, not in the abstract,
but as a real involvement with the people who actually suffer *injustice*."[41] "It is a fact," Arrupe wrote in 1966, "that the Society is

not sufficiently orientated towards social justice; rather, it always has been focused, in accordance with a strategy justified mainly by historical conditions, toward exercising an impact on the dominant social classes, and in the training of their leaders."[42]

This arresting challenge to a group of priests who had by then settled into the relatively comfortable task of leading colleges and universities around the world was followed shortly thereafter by the Society's collective declaration at its Thirty-Second General Congregation that "our apostolate today urgently requires that we [commit ourselves to the promotion of justice]. . . . For us, the promotion of justice is not one apostolic area among many others, the 'social apostolate.' Rather, it should be the concern of our whole life, and a dimension of all our apostolic endeavors."[43] This category of "all" obviously included the educational apostolate in which most Jesuits in the United States were engaged. And therein lay the controversy. It is one thing to dedicate oneself and one's efforts to the "service of faith and the promotion of justice" when one is manning a soup kitchen in the Bronx, a reservation in South Dakota, or even a parish in suburbia. But how about if one is the president of Georgetown or Fordham or Boston College? How does one promote justice in the shaping of curriculum, the granting of tenure, and the carrying out of independent scholarship?

According to Ignacio Ellacuría and his colleagues at the UCA, one simply takes the words of the General Congregation to heart and applies them to the institutional, social, and political circumstances in which one finds oneself. For example, the Thirty-Second Congregation, in its oft-cited chapter 4, had pronounced that "our faith in Christ Jesus and our mission to proclaim the Gospel demand of us a commitment to promote justice and to enter into solidarity with the voiceless and the powerless." What could be a more relevant rallying cry to men who saw themselves as using their university in San Salvador to advance and continue the work of an archbishop who referred to himself as the "voice of the voiceless"? "We can not be excused," the Thirty-Second Congregation stated, "from making the most rigorous possible political and social analysis of our situations." So how could the Jesuits of El Salvador do anything but devote their university to analysis of a situation in their country that was dire in the extreme? Moreover "an effort to promote justice," according to the Thirty-Second General Congregation, "will cost us something. Our cheerful readiness to pay the price will make our preaching of the Gospel more meaningful and its acceptance easier."[44] This was an enduring inspiration for a Salvadoran community that had paid a high price already in the blood of Rutilio Grande, the martyrdom of Oscar Romero, and the violent opposition to their educational activities shown by a government that accused them of serving as the intellectual agitators of a leftist revolution.

When viewed in these terms, it is wholly unsurprising that the Jesuit leaders of the UCA pursued the course they pursued. And it is equally unsurprising that the governing authorities viewed that course as being deeply subversive of the public order. It *was* subversive of the public order. The Jesuits at the UCA were not the instigators of the revolt, nor were they anything like the uncritical supporters of the FMLN that the Salvadoran authorities accused them of being. In fact, the priests decried the violence of the revolutionary forces, and they devoted themselves to advocating a peaceful negotiation of the conflict. But they did not shy away from the task of promoting justice, and they made no excuses for offering "rigorous political and social analysis of [their] situation," in the words of the Thirty-Second Congregation. Indeed, Ellacuría and his colleagues noted often that they were prepared to pay the price for doing what they were doing. For they were convinced that what they were doing was what they were duty-bound to do—as Christians, as priests, but most especially as Jesuits.

In addition, Ellacuría also felt duty-bound to remind his fellow Jesuits outside of El Salvador, and especially in the United States, that this was the kind of thing to which they were supposed to be devoting their universities as well, according to their own context and their own possibilities. And as indicated above, that challenge intersected with a debate within the United States over the proper mission and role of Jesuit universities. Paul Locatelli, then the president of Santa Clara University and a forceful proponent of the responsibility of Jesuit universities to "the service of faith and the promotion of justice," invited Ellacuría to receive an honorary degree at his university in California's Silicon Valley in 1982. The speech that the Salvadoran rector gave on that occasion was an eloquent statement of one very passionately held position of what should distinguish a Jesuit university.[45]

A Jesuit university, Ellacuría stated, "must transform and enlighten the society in which it lives." It must, in other words, "do everything possible so that liberty is victorious over oppression, justice over injustice, love over hate." And how is this done? It is done by committing the means that are "uniquely at [a university's] disposal." In an oft-quoted passage, Ellacuría outlined a mission statement for any Jesuit university that might be looking for one:

> We as an intellectual community must analyze causes; use imagination and creativity together to discover the remedies of our problems; communicate to our constituencies a consciousness that inspires the freedom of self-determination; educate professionals with a conscience, who will be the immediate instruments of such a transformation; and constantly hone an educational institution that is both academically excellent and ethically oriented. . . . A Christian university must take into account the gospel preference for the poor. This does not mean that only the poor will study at the university. . . . What it does mean is that the university should be present intellectually where it is needed: to provide science for those without science; to provide skills for those without skills; to be a voice for those without voices; to give intellectual support for those who do not possess the academic qualifications to make their rights legitimate.

Referring specifically to his own experience at the UCA, Ellacuría said at Santa Clara that "[the UCA's] work is oriented, obviously, on behalf of our Salvadoran culture, but above all, on behalf of a people who, oppressed by structural injustices, struggle for their self-determination—people often without liberty or human rights. . . . But," he added significantly, "American universities also have an important part to play in order to insure that the unavoidable presence of the United States in Central America be sensitive and just, *especially those universities—like Santa Clara—which are inspired by the desire to make present among us all the Kingdom of God*" (emphasis added).

I have quoted this speech at length for two reasons. The first, again, is that Ellacuría was then in person, as he still is now in memory, a particularly outspoken advocate for the idea that Jesuit universities, regardless of where they find themselves, should carry out the specifically Jesuit mission of serving faith in the promotion of justice. But the second reason that I have quoted him at such length is to give the reader some idea of who this man was, and with what ideas and commitments he was associated among Jesuits in the United States in the 1980s. The Ignacio Ellacuría who issued such a challenge to American "universities which are [ostensibly!] inspired by the desire to make present among us all the Kingdom of God" is the same Ignacio Ellacuría who was roused in the middle of the night and executed with a bullet in the back of the head by an army that was receiving the bulk of its funding from the US taxpayer. Moreover, he was killed because he was doing exactly what he had challenged his North American brothers to do. He was, as the president of a Jesuit university, trying to "transform and enlighten the society in which it lives." No wonder O'Hare at Fordham, Monan at Boston College, O'Donovan at Georgetown, and all the rest of the presidents of Jesuit universities spread out across US society were so particularly horrified by the murders at the UCA. Their brothers had been killed with bullets bought by their government precisely because the Salvadoran Jesuits had refused to content themselves with merely "exercising an impact on the dominant social classes and in the training of their leaders" (as Arrupe said in 1966). That event was such a direct challenge to Jesuits in the United States, on so many different levels, that they could not help but respond with all of the resources at their disposal.

Solidarity

The resources at the Jesuits' disposal were substantial, as was made clear from the very beginning. The less obvious point was the degree to which those resources could be translated into influence over two closely related phenomena: the judicial system of El Salvador, and the foreign policy of the US government. The first indicator of the fervor with which Jesuits in the United States responded to the assassinations at the UCA was the public outpouring of outrage outlined at the beginning of this chapter. But the second was the decision by Jesuits in the United States to associate themselves publicly with a woman named Lucia Barrera de Cerna, the only witness to the actual crime ever to come forward in El Salvador.[46] Cerna was a housekeeper at the Jesuit residence at the UCA who was staying that night in a house adjacent to the campus. She was awakened by loud voices in the yard next to the Jesuits' house, went to her window, and saw at least five men dressed in what she said were the distinctive uniforms of the Salvadoran army. Paralyzed with fear, she crouched by the window and listened as the soldiers woke the priests and gathered them in the yard. She heard the exchanges between the two groups of men grow more intense and ominous as the interaction progressed from intrusion to murder. At first the priests asked the intruders to lower their voices. The army had searched the UCA before (just two nights earlier, for example), and presumably that is what the Jesuits thought was the purpose of this visit as well. But soon darker intentions became apparent, and Cerna heard Martín-Baró denounce the soldiers as "scum" and their intentions as "an outrage." The last sound of the priests' voices was a hushed unison—in what Cerna assumed was communal prayer—before that prayer was drowned out and cut off by five single gunshots, one immediately following the other.[47]

Lucia Cerna did not actually see soldiers of the Atlacatl Battalion execute the Jesuit priests. But she knew the battalion by sight, and she knew the Jesuits by voice, and she was certain, without actually seeing the shots fired, that Ellacuría, Montes, Martín-Baró, López y López, Moreno, and López had been killed by a unit of the Salvadoran military. And in a move of great courage, she indicated such immediately, the following morning, to the Jesuit provincial, José María Tojeira. Tojeira lived at another Jesuit residence just a few hundred yards from where the murders had taken place, and he served as the central representative of the Society of Jesus, both at the site that morning and throughout the ensuing struggle to bring what he himself called the "intellectual authors of the crime" to justice. Tojeira's first step on hearing Cerna's account was to introduce her to María Julia Hernández, director of the archdiocese's legal aid office. Hernández, in turn, recognized the account as explosive testimony, and she arranged for Cerna to testify immediately in front of the judge who had been assigned to investigate the case. She also arranged for Cerna and her family to be flown out of El Salvador to ensure their safety.

Details of these events are complex and contested, but several facts are clear. Lucia Cerna and her family were brought by Tojeira and Hernández to the Spanish embassy (flying the Salvadoran flag momentarily to ensure the legality and legitimacy of her testimony), where on November 22 she began to testify before Judge Ricardo Zamora. Over the course of the next day, discussions ensued between Tojeira and the US embassy concerning when Cerna and her family would leave El Salvador for Miami, who would accompany them, and what would happen to them when they arrived in Florida. In the end, Tojeira agreed that the family would be accompanied by an official from the embassy (ostensibly to aid their passage through customs and immigration) and that they would be turned over to Jesuits in the United States immediately upon their arrival.

What actually happened, however, was that Cerna was held in isolation in Miami for four days while she was questioned not only by officials from the US embassy in El Salvador but also by officers of the Salvadoran army itself. After repetitive rounds of what she took to be threatening questions, she recanted, claimed to know nothing about the murders at the UCA, and then—but only on the basis of her recantation—failed a series of lie detector tests about her testimony. Her new claim that she had seen nothing, along with the lie detector results, was presented by everyone from President Christiani to US Ambassador Walker as evidence that Cerna was an unstable and unreliable witness.[48] She recanted. She failed a lie detector test. These were presented as reasons not to believe her original testimony, when in fact she recanted only when threatened by Salvadoran army officers. And she failed a lie detector test about the recantation itself, not about her original testimony.

Tojeira and his colleagues in San Salvador were outraged at the manipulation of Lucia Cerna, and relations between the Jesuits and the US embassy were damaged by what the Jesuits saw as an uncon-scionable double-cross of a vulnerable and frightened witness.[49] But the Jesuits in El Salvador were joined in their outrage by the Jesuits in the United States when they were finally allowed to "take custody" of the witness and her family. She immediately told them of her ordeal and readily restated with emphasis that she *had* seen the sol-diers on the UCA campus that night, and she *was* certain that they were the "scum" who had committed the "outrage."[50] The American Jesuit most involved in this process was the late Paul Tipton, who was at the time the president of the Association of Jesuit Colleges and Universities. Tipton flew to Miami, swept Cerna and her family off to a safe and hidden location (in Alabama, as it turned out), and began a public relations campaign to draw attention to the treat-ment of the witness specifically and to the US government's acqui-escence in the cover-up of the murders more generally.

The complex dynamic surrounding the attempted burning of the witness is important for two reasons. The first is that it indi-cated the degree to which the Jesuits in the United States had in-stitutional resources at their disposal. Tipton took the lead in the name of the AJCU. But he was also joined by Richard Buhler of the Jesuit Conference, yet another institutional arm of the Jesuits, this one tasked to oversee and coordinate the activities and interests of the ten Jesuit provinces within the United States. Twenty-eight colleges and universities, ten provinces and provincials—this was a lot of institutions in a lot of places, with regular access to journal-ists and politicians. The second important point, however, was the effect that the US embassy's complicity in the treatment of Lucia Cerna had on Jesuit attitudes and Jesuit expressions of solidarity in the United States. Charlie Beirne later told Ambassador Walker to his face that if Walker did not know that the murders had been ordered by the Salvadoran army, he was incompetent, and that if he did know and did nothing about it, then he was something worse—an accomplice.[51] But even many Jesuits who were not actually in El Salvador and who did not share Beirne's confrontational style were radicalized by the eye-opening events in Miami.

There was a witness who had convincingly implicated the Sal-vadoran army in the murder of their brothers. And the Salvadoran government had gone to obviously manipulative lengths to discredit that witness. But much worse, from the point of view of Tipton, Buhler, and their Jesuit colleagues across the country, was the fact that the US government had aided the Salvadorans in that attempt. This led many Jesuits to ask whose side "we" were on in El Salvador: the murdered or the murderers. More fundamentally, it led many Jesuits in the United States to ask who "we" actually were in such a circumstance, where the interests of the US government and the interests of the Society of Jesus so sharply diverged? Were they Jesuits, they asked themselves, or were they American citizens? The obvious answer was that they were powerfully rooted in both identities. And a large number of American Jesuits resolved, on the basis of the treatment of Lucia Barrera de Cerna, that they would have to pressure the American government as Americans if they were going to bring about justice in the Jesuit case as Jesuits.

Relieving the Debt

The first step, however, involved matters that are best defined as institutional in nature. When the group of presidents of the US Jesuit universities visited San Salvador in February 1990, one of their brother Jesuits they met with was Francisco "Paco" Estrada, who had just been named to replace Ellacuría as rector of the UCA. Hoping to offer something more concrete than an expression of solidarity, or to provide some measure of indirect physical protection, the group that included O'Hare from Fordham and Monan from Boston College asked how they could help. Estrada recalled in an interview with me that this request came just as he was seething over an insulting gesture by the US embassy to create a fund at the UCA in the name of Ignacio Ellacuría in the paltry amount of one thousand dollars. Estrada was already furious at what he perceived to be the embassy's complicity in the cover-up of the crime; now he was also appalled that the US government, in the name of the embassy, would offer so little to the UCA at a time of such great crisis. Struck by the irony that US citizens were now asking him how they could help him at the UCA, he recalled, still with pleasure two decades later, that an idea hit him immediately. If the American Jesuits wanted to help, there actually was something very concrete that they could do. They could persuade the US government to help the UCA get out from under a crushing debt that was threatening to destroy the university, or at least erode its independence.[52]

The financial details are complex and a bit arcane, but the basic facts were that the UCA had secured some years before a substantial loan from the Inter-American Development Bank (IDB) to help in rebuilding both the physical plant and the curriculum of the university.[53] The problem was that in the ensuing years, the US dollar had appreciated against the Salvadoran *corona*, and the IDB was insisting in 1990 on receiving its payment for the loan in dollars. The UCA administrators had borrowed and spent *coronas*; now they were being told they had to pay back ten million US dollars, and they did not have anywhere near that amount of money available. Two possibilities, neither of them acceptable, faced Estrada when he took over the UCA just a week after the murders. The IDB could call in the loan, thereby foreclosing on the university and either shutting it down or decimating its operations. Or the Salvadoran government could step in and pay the debt and through that action take control of the UCA, reconfigure its administration and faculty, and in effect rescind the educational mission for which the six Jesuits had just given their lives. But if the US government could somehow erase the loan, then the UCA could retain its independence and move forward from the trauma of the assassinations with at least the chance of institutional recovery and renewal on the horizon.

Paco Estrada's request was practical and canny, but it was also controversial. It would not do for the US government simply to pay a $10 million debt for a Salvadoran university. That would be problematic in both procedural and political terms for the US government. But a direct subsidy from the US government would also be awkward for the leadership of the UCA itself. Fordham's O'Hare recalled the sensitive dynamics: "We had to figure out a way that the debt could be relieved without it appearing that the UCA was receiving money directly from a US government that was being denounced in El Salvador for supporting the Salvadoran Army."[54] The job of working out these details and navigating the political sensitivities on all sides fell to Paul Tipton at the AJCU in Washington and to Charlie Beirne in his new post as vice-rector at the UCA. Beirne made a number of trips to Washington over the next year or so to consult with Tipton and other Jesuits and to lobby directly on Capitol Hill on behalf of the UCA. What transpired in the end was that the US Congress appropriated a specially earmarked grant of $10 million to the Salvadoran government that was understood by all parties to free up money that could be used to pay the IDB on behalf of the UCA, no strings attached. In effect the US Jesuits, acting on Estrada's request, got their own US government to fund an opportunity for the UCA to start anew after the murders, with a clean financial slate and on a much firmer financial footing. Without that opportunity, all concerned—both in the United States and in El Salvador—are convinced even today that the UCA may not have survived as the university that Ellacuría and his martyred colleagues had built.

The Moakley Commission

During the same trip to El Salvador in February 1990, the Jesuit presidents had bumped into a group of congressional staff members who were in the country in advance of a visit shortly thereafter by a delegation from the US Congress that would come to be known as the Moakley Commission. Joseph Moakley, a US representative from Boston (D-MA), had been appointed by Speaker Thomas Foley in the immediate aftermath of the deaths at the UCA to lead a small group of members of the House who would oversee the prosecution of the Jesuit case and make recommendations to Speaker Foley and to Congress on the basis of their findings. Moakley was a surprising, but as it turned out inspired, choice for this post. Chairman of the powerful Rules Committee and very well connected in the internal networks of the House of Representatives, Moakley had virtually no direct experience in foreign policy, much less in the complexities involved in the web of political-military relations in a place like El Salvador. Nevertheless, Moakley and his top aide, Jim McGovern, threw themselves into the task with enormous energy and commitment, and over the next couple of years they became the most painful thorn in the side of the Salvadoran and US governments when it came to investigation of the Jesuit murders.

US Jesuits played an important but limited role in the work of the Moakley Commission. They met with Moakley and McGovern and mapped out for them the nature of relations between the Jesuits and the Salvadoran government. They cooperated with the Commission throughout, coordinating parallel efforts to pressure the Salvadoran government to prosecute the case and to convince the US Congress to cut off military aid to the Salvadoran army that had murdered the six Jesuits in cold blood at the UCA. And they relied on Moakley's good offices (literally, in the sense that Charlie Beirne worked out of Moakley's office when he was in Washington) in the work they were doing in Congress to solve the debt problem for Paco Estrada and the university. But it really was Moakley and McGovern—along with Martha Doggett, an investigator sent to El Salvador by the Lawyers Committee on Human Rights to advise and represent Tojeira and the Salvadoran Jesuits—who did the important work of keeping pressure on the Salvadoran and US governments regarding the case and also of managing to keep the case on the pages of American newspapers.

Here is not the place for a detailed account of Moakley's tireless work on the case, nor of Doggett's skill and sensitivity in navigating the Salvadoran judicial system. Both have received ample documentation elsewhere.[55] Suffice it to point out simply that Moakley's commitment was motivated by a personal realization that was for him fairly straightforward and obvious. He was, as he liked to remind people, an old-fashioned congressman. He thought his job was to advance the interests of the people in his district, and he did that job well. He was, one could argue, more interested in pork than in policy. But the more Moakley looked into what had happened in El Salvador, and the more he discovered that the Salvadoran regime was deeply implicated in the crime, the more tenacious he became. This army that the United States was supporting in El Salvador was not only an army that was murdering innocent victims, although that was bad enough. This was an army that was executing innocent *priests* in cold blood, for God's sake. That was not a very complicated thing in the mind of an Irish Catholic politician from South Boston who had attended Catholic schools and who had represented other Catholic citizens in Congress for years. It was simple—and it was simply wrong. Boston College was in Moakley's district; he knew Donald Monan and other Jesuits personally. The murders at the UCA and the cover-up in El Salvador were the kind of circumstances that could motivate a patronage pol to devote years of his congressional service to influencing American foreign policy towards a small Central American nation.

The Jesuit Family

No other member of Congress was as devoted to the Jesuit case as Moakley was. But many other senators and representatives did take a particular interest in the case, and a relatively large number related the case immediately and directly to an issue that had been on the congressional agenda for years: military aid to the Salvadoran regime. Senator Patrick Leahy (D-VT), for example, who was himself a graduate of Georgetown Law School and who had been trying to get Congress to cut off aid to the Salvadoran army for years before 1989, said in exasperation a few days after the murders: "If now is not the time, what in Heaven's name has to happen in that country before it is the time?"[56] Senator Chris Dodd (D-CT), who had attended Georgetown Prep with the Jesuits as a schoolboy, dropped his opposition to Leahy's efforts after the outlines of a cover-up became clear, and Dodd also became an outspoken critic of US policy in El Salvador. As Teresa Whitfield put it in her discussion of the policy debates at the time, congressional debate was ongoing but inconclusive concerning the propriety of funding the Salvadoran military—"and then came the Jesuits."[57]

That phrase, "and then came the Jesuits," can be taken in two ways. Whitfield meant it in the sense of "and then the Jesuits were murdered." But we can also understand it in terms of "and then the Jesuits opposed US policy in El Salvador." That opposition was immediate, forceful, and relatively influential. Luis Calero happened to be in New Orleans with the prominent peace activist and fellow Jesuit Daniel Berrigan when they received the news of the murders.

Calero recalled that their immediate response was to organize a protest calling for the suspension of US aid to the Salvadoran military.[58]
This reaction was common among the Jesuits in the United States,
although not all of them took up placards in protest. Instead they all
did what they could in their particular circumstances to advance the
goal of suspending aid. Luis Calero and Dan Berrigan marched in
New Orleans. President O'Donovan of Georgetown University met
with Assistant Secretary of State Lawrence Eagleburger in Washington.[59] President Locatelli of Santa Clara University called and met
with Representative Leon Panetta (D-CA), a Santa Clara alumnus
who was then the chairman of the House Budget Committee, and
told him that now was the time to change policy in El Salvador.[60] All
of the Jesuits with whom I discussed these matters did something
similar. Many of them were local figures of some prominence in
their communities: Boston, Washington, San Francisco, and so on.
They knew members of Congress personally; they had lobbied those
members before, often on issues of institutional significance to their
colleges and universities. Now they called their contacts, leveraged
their connections, on an issue of much greater personal importance.
Across the country Jesuits contacted members of Congress and told
them that the US government had to stop funding a military force
that was guilty of murdering their brothers in El Salvador.

It has been wisely said that trying to specify influence on legisla-
tion is like trying to identify a black cat in a garbage can at night. But
what we can do here by way of suggesting the influence of the Jesuits
on US policy is emphasize two things: first, the claim made by many
members of Congress that they were deeply affected not only by the
murders themselves but also by the reaction to them by the Jesuits
in the United States; and second, the timing of congressional action.

Typical of the statements made by members of Congress were
the words of Representative Don Edwards (D-CA), who informed
the House of "Father Ellacuría's strong ties" to Edwards's Bay Area
district through "Ellacuría's association with Santa Clara University," and who entered into the *Congressional Record* an article in the
San Jose Mercury News by Jesuits at Santa Clara mourning the Salvadoran martyrs, and calling for a cessation of US military funding
in response.[61] Senator Daniel Patrick Moynihan (D-NY) did a very

similar thing, recounting a personal meeting he had had with Ellacuría and Martín-Baró some years before, placing Leo O'Donovan's
Washington Post op-ed article denouncing the murders of the Jesuit
brothers into the *Congressional Record*, and reminding his Senate
colleagues in passionate terms this was a "murder which most likely
was carried out with American weapons. May I say that again? A
massacre which was most likely carried out with American supplied
weapons."[62]

Representative Nancy Pelosi (D-CA), whose district includes the
Jesuit University of San Francisco, framed the influence of the "Jesuit family" on Congress in even broader terms. "Many of us in this
body," she said on the floor of the House, "belong to the Jesuit family; either we have brothers, sisters, or children who have been educated by the Jesuits, and know the close ties that bind. . . . We have
been hearing from those of the Jesuit family throughout the country," she continued, "to call for a cease fire, for a negotiated settlement, for an investigation into the slayings and a second look again
at our policy in El Salvador which has not diminished the violence
and which we have an opportunity to do."[63] Senator Brock Adams
(D-WA) heard directly from actual, vowed members of the "Jesuit
family." At the end of his speech calling on Congress to "stop aiding
and abetting this tragedy," he placed in the *Congressional Record* a
letter to him from forty Jesuits at Gonzaga University in his home
state of Washington, imploring "the government to stop shipment
of all arms to El Salvador."[64]

The *Congressional Record* is filled with actions such as these and
rhetoric such as this. I cited Mohammed Ahrari in the introductory
chapter, noting his point that the influence of ethnic lobbying on
policy is determined in part by the congruence of the lobby's ethnic
interests with US strategic interests in the country under consideration.[65] Obviously, the Jesuits' transnational communal interests
were diametrically opposed to the strategic interests of the George
H. W. Bush administration in El Salvador in 1989 and 1990. Foreign
policy, however, and the articulation through policy of US strategic
interests are more complicated than a simple reflection of executive
preference or presidential will. What made the Jesuits' insistence
on a change in policy in El Salvador so significant at this particular

juncture is that their insistence, and the murders that inspired it, provided a graphic justification for opposition to American foreign policy that was already percolating in Congress. The murders at the UCA, and the mobilization of the United States–based Jesuits in response to them, did not create opposition to US policy in El Salvador. Instead those shocking events and the Jesuits' mobilization in response provided a hook onto which members of Congress could hang their already growing reservations about continuing support for the Salvadoran military.

Representative Moakley, the member of Congress who followed these matters more closely than any other official in Washington, was sure that the tumult raised by the Jesuits had profoundly affected US policy in El Salvador. Referring specifically to the growing movement to cut off military aid, Moakley said in 1990 that "the Jesuit murders were the thing that did it. . . . Had not the killings happened . . . had not the Jesuits themselves and a lot of upset Americans stuck with this issue, then the aid would still be flowing like mother's milk."[66] The murders revealed for many in Congress the true nature of the regime that the United States was supporting. And that realization was encouraged by the Jesuits, directly through lobbying and advocacy and indirectly by what we might call the untapped political capital of the "Jesuit family."

Roman Catholics made up at the time the largest single religious grouping in the US Congress; and as Representative Pelosi pointed out, some of the most prominent of those members—Leahy, Dodd, Panetta, and others—had a direct connection to the Jesuits through their own experiences at Jesuit educational institutions. Partly as a response to these connections, military aid to El Salvador was cut in half in 1990. It was then restored by President George H. W. Bush in 1991, but that restoration came as part of a policy designed to keep the Salvadoran military at the negotiating table. Finally, everything changed with the signing of the peace accord between the Salvadoran government and the FMLN in 1992. The political dynamic surrounding the issue of military aid was no less complex and contested after November 1989 than it had been before. But the involvement of the Society of Jesus altered that dynamic substantially. To repeat, with Whitfield, "and then came the Jesuits."[67]

What Happened Next?

The ramifications of the Jesuit case were varied and profound. For one thing, the trial that took place in San Salvador was an unusually revealing look into the workings of the Salvadoran justice system.[68] It was clear from the very beginning that President Christiani's government and the Salvadoran military were engaged in either a mass cover-up to prevent the crime from being prosecuted at all or a well-designed campaign to manage the proceedings so that critics, particularly in the United States and within the Society of Jesus, could be mollified without the arm of the law ever reaching into the higher echelons of the military. The Salvadoran government resisted from the very beginning any implication that the killings at the UCA had been ordered by the military's high command. Christiani did admit in the early days that the shootings bore the earmarks of the Salvadoran armed forces.[69] Even he, in other words, did not try to perpetuate the absurd initial claim that the Jesuits had been killed by the FMLN.[70] But after a fairly high ranking officer, Colonel Guillermo Alfredo Benavides, was given up, any other attempts to follow the trail of guilt toward the top of the chain of command were vigorously resisted.[71]

Perhaps even more telling, in terms of establishing the illegitimacy of the judicial proceedings, was the fact that the jury's verdict in the trial that followed was an absurdity in itself. Colonel Benavides, several of his lieutenants, and five enlisted men of the Atlacatl Battalion were all tried for the murders of the priests. Indeed the enlisted men who served as the actual triggermen at the killings had confessed their guilt and had described the scene in grisly and chilling detail.[72] In the end, however, the jury found only Colonel Benavides guilty of all the murders, while convicting Lieutenant Yusshy Mendoza (who was actually on the scene) only of killing Celina Ramos, the teenage daughter of the priests' cook. "Where is the outrage?" asked Representative Moakley in an article in the *Washington Post*, decrying what he saw as the US government's silent acquiescence in the "terrible injustice" represented by the trial.[73]

Where was the outrage? Well, there was plenty of outrage among the Jesuits in the United States. Donald Monan, who had attended the trial and witnessed the verdict (as always to show solidarity with the Salvadoran Jesuits and to "represent the American [Jesuit] institutions"), was totally outraged by what he had witnessed.[74] So was Charlie Beirne, who two decades later still smarted at the fact that no one who was actually at the UCA on the night of November 16, 1989, was convicted for killing the Jesuits. His voice still dripping with outrage, Beirne argued in an interview with me that the verdicts were an exercise in cynicism. "Apparently, killing the housekeeper was okay," he said, "because she had been working with the Jesuits, and therefore she got what she deserved."[75] What the verdict said, in clear terms, was that the only innocent person killed at the UCA that night was Elena Ramos's daughter, Celina. Only she had had nothing directly to do with the troublemakers before their deaths.

Monan and Beirne's dismissal of the trial as a miscarriage of justice was supported by a report issued in 1993 by a UN truth commission that examined the atrocities committed during the Salvadoran Civil War. The report, titled *From Madness to Hope*, asserted the guilt of the entire high command of the Salvadoran military in the Jesuit case. It specifically identified Colonel René Emilio Ponce (who was promoted to general and named minister of defense *after* the murders), General Juan Rafael Bustillo (who was chief of the Salvadoran Air Force at the time of the murders and later ran for president), and Colonels Juan Orlando Zepeda, Inocente Orlando Montano, and Francisco Elena Fuentes as the officers who had ordered Colonel Benavides to use soldiers of the Atlacatl Battalion to eliminate Ellacuría and "to leave no witnesses."[76] In short, the United Nations ratified what Tojeira had said immediately after the bodies were discovered. The murders at the UCA were not a rogue operation; they were a disciplined military action carried out in response to direct orders issued by top military officers who had been working closely for years with the US embassy. The intellectual authors of the crime had been identified. They were the entire high command of the Salvadoran military.

As I indicate at the very beginning of this chapter, however, the military leaders had acted on a serious miscalculation in killing Ellacuría and his colleagues. Virtually no one believed their original

cover story that the FMLN had committed the murders to eliminate Ellacuría's advocacy for a negotiated settlement. And in time
the generals and colonels who had acted so brutally for so long and
with so much impunity were cited in public as having killed the
priests. But perhaps even worse than that outcome, from the point
of view of those generals and colonels, was that the killings at the
UCA set in motion a series of political developments that led in
time to the very outcome that Ellacuría had been assassinated for
advocating: a negotiated peace agreement between the government
of El Salvador and the guerillas.

Again, there are always complex reasons for political outcomes.[77]
We would not want to reduce the peace accords in El Salvador to
a response to the deaths at the UCA. And it would be difficult to
establish such a claim in any rigorous way, given the impossibil-
ity of testing it against plausible alternative explanations through
comparison with other comparable cases. The dramatic shifts in international politics that were taking place at the time surely played
a role, as the Soviet Union collapsed and political alignments and
circumstances changed all over the world. US attention was turning away from Central America, in part as a result of the end of
the Cold War, and was focusing more pointedly on places like the
Middle East where vital US economic interests were at stake. And
inside El Salvador we should not minimize the role that sheer military exhaustion played in bringing the two sides to the table. Peace
in El Salvador, one might say using social science terminology, was
overdetermined.

But that is not to deny that the killing of the Jesuits backfired
on the military, or that the death of the Jesuits deeply influenced
the course of events that led to the signing of the peace accords in
February 1992. That influence ranged from the very concrete, in
the effect of the assassinations on congressional support for continued military aid, to the more symbolic, such as the FMLN's call
for a cease-fire to begin on the night of November 16, 1991, the
second anniversary of the murders.[78] I agree with Teresa Whitfield,
who wrote in her book *Paying the Price* that the deaths at the UCA
had "catalyzed the reinitiation of negotiations. . . . The case had
kept the army on the defensive," she added, and "had consistently

contributed to the change in U.S. policy that allowed negotiations to prosper."[79] We do not have to satisfy ourselves, however, with accepting Whitfield's retrospective judgment that widespread "revulsion" at the killings had served as a "trigger" for the political changes that led to the peace accord. We can just as easily credit the opinion of a high-ranking Salvadoran officer who upbraided his colleagues at the military's operations center for celebrating Ellacuría's death on the morning after the killings. "Idiots!" shouted Colonel Roberto Pineda Guerra, on November 17, 1989. "Don't you realize we have just lost the war?"[80]

Conclusion

The central point for the purpose of this book is that all of the political actions undertaken by the Jesuits in the United States were so distinctively derived from the specific nature of the transnational Jesuit community. The many reactions to the murders at the UCA and the actions that flowed from them all grew directly out of the particular form of transnationalism embodied by the Society of Jesus and out of the specific mission and charism of the Jesuit community.

The Jesuits in the United States responded to the deaths of their brothers in El Salvador in a remarkably communal and active way. As Richard Buhler, then of the Jesuit Conference in Washington, DC, put it, "These deaths touched Jesuits everywhere in a way that no single other event in the Salvadoran war seems to have done."[81] Jesuits in the United States had already been shocked by the brazen murder of Oscar Romero. They had joined in the mourning of the four American churchwomen who had been raped and killed in San Salvador later in 1980. But the murders at the UCA in 1989 were different, infinitely more personal, and they struck at the very heart of a distinctively Jesuit mode of belonging. Ellacuría and the other martyrs in El Salvador had performed the Spiritual Exercises just as Jesuits in the United States had done. They all answered to the same father general in Rome, and they all participated in the same web of meetings and conferences and congregations that gave the order its form.

If the effectiveness of transnational political solidarity is determined in part by the degree of homogeneity exhibited within the transnational community itself, then the Society of Jesus was an excellent candidate for effective action. Ellacuría and the other Salvadoran martyrs differed from their brother Jesuits in the United States in many ways. But the most important thing, more important than any cultural or national divide, was that they were brother Jesuits. It was obvious why the murders at the UCA had touched all the Jesuits in such a deep and meaningful way. Six of their own had been murdered, and it was central to the Society's fraternal ethos that other Jesuits would feel a communal responsibility to act in the name of brothers who had been harmed by outsiders.

Moreover, the forms that those actions took were also particular to the structures that defined the Jesuit community in the United States and to the position that Jesuit priests occupied in American society. Jesuits in the United States responded to the murder of their brothers in ways that were straightforwardly political and that squarely targeted what political scientists call the elite level of political action. There were some public demonstrations, and there were some efforts to widen the web of solidarity in the United States. But the basic approach of the Jesuits was to turn to their contacts in the corridors of power, to speak from positions of institutional influence, and to seek direct access to political leaders in both Washington and San Salvador. There was not really all that much that was contemplative about it. In Jesuit parlance, contemplation was for the purpose of discernment, and discernment was to lead swiftly to action.

There was a certain inescapable irony about all of this, of course. Recall Pedro Arrupe's lament that the Jesuits had for too long contented themselves with seeking only to influence the "dominant social classes," primarily through the "training of their leaders." The basic truth of the matter was that the exercise of that traditional role was what had provided the Jesuits with access to the dominant class in Washington in the first place. And the Jesuits relied on that access to local and national political elites as their primary lever of influence when their brothers were murdered—precisely because they had eschewed that traditional role in favor of the pursuit of justice among the poor in El Salvador.

Most importantly, virtually all of the political activities undertaken by Jesuits in the United States in response to the murders were grounded in one way or another in the twenty-eight Jesuit colleges and universities across the country. The entire dynamic, in Charlie Beirne's word, was conducted *universidadamente*. In one sense, this was merely because academia is where most Jesuits in the United States found themselves in 1989. Their leadership of colleges and universities was what gave them standing in their particular communities, access to the local media, and, such as it was, influence in Congress. But the extent to which their political response was grounded in universities went deeper than just this logistical level. As Buhler also said at the time, "As an order of scholars, [the Jesuits] also took [the murders at the UCA] as an attack on intellectual freedom as much as on the church."[82] For Jesuit professors and administrators in the United States, it was not just that the Salvadorans were fellow members of the Society, although that was plenty of motivation in itself. It was also that these Salvadoran Jesuits were engaged in the same educational apostolate as their American brothers at Georgetown, Fordham, and the rest, and that the Salvadorans had been killed for carrying out that apostolate with such commitment and sacrifice. Of course, that connection was woven even deeper by the fact that Ignacio Ellacuría, in word and deed, had offered such an eloquent challenge to his colleagues in the United States to strengthen their own commitment to the Jesuit mission—to dedicate their own institutions of higher learning to the service of faith in the promotion of justice.

I began this chapter by describing the rose garden at the UCA as a site of pilgrimage for people who come to El Salvador to gain a deeper and more visceral understanding of the struggles that define the Catholic Church in El Salvador. I now want to end by pointing out a more metaphorical pilgrimage that also places the UCA at the center. Jesuits in the United States continue to struggle over the tensions between influencing the "dominant social classes" through the "training of their leaders," in Arrupe's words, and serving Christian faith through the promotion of justice. Given the status of places like Georgetown University and Boston College, and given the clarity and centrality of the Society's expressed mission, resolving these tensions and navigating the path to a new educational apostolate are not easy tasks. Nevertheless, navigating that path is now one of the central challenges faced by presidents of the Jesuit colleges and universities in the United States. I have interviewed many of them; they all talk about that task readily, and they all describe themselves as struggling with it mightily. And as a result, for many of these presidents (and of course, many of their faculty colleagues), the UCA and the Jesuit martyrs have become a kind of central metaphor of an effort to reorient their institutions away from the traditional role of training the children of the dominant classes and toward a more explicit pursuit of justice.

For example, I attended the inauguration of Charles Beirne as president of LeMoyne College in Syracuse, New York. The decorations and iconography were entirely Central American, and the rhetoric was full of references to justice and responsibility and to the examples of the martyrs at the UCA. I interviewed President Steven Privett in his office at the University of San Francisco, a man whose own inauguration address was grounded entirely in the example of the UCA.[83] His office is practically a shrine to the martyrs, a self-consciously public expression of his insistence that the university ground itself in its local reality of San Francisco and devote itself to educating the children of the city in the promotion of social justice.

Finally, I spent several days at Santa Clara University, an institution that is, through the tireless efforts of its former president Locatelli, generally recognized as the fulcrum of connection between the UCA and the Jesuit universities in the United States. The memory of the martyrs is everywhere at Santa Clara. There are eight crosses on the lawn of the chapel, bearing the names of the six Jesuits, their cook, and her daughter. A plaque inside the student service offices of the university names and dedicates the space to Elba and Celina Ramos. A program regularly sends faculty to San Salvador to visit the UCA, to speak with faculty there, and to deepen their own understanding of how Santa Clara University, the self-proclaimed "Jesuit

University in the Silicon Valley," can make its own unique contribution to the service of faith and the promotion of justice. Finally,
there is a small office at Santa Clara University that administers a
program called Casa Solidaridad in San Salvador. The brain child
of Dean Brackley, Casa Solidaridad is a study-abroad program that
sends to El Salvador fifteen to twenty students each semester from
various Jesuit colleges and universities around the United States.
While their friends from home might choose to study for a semester
in London, Paris, or some other equally captivating European city,
these students, being educated in what is always termed "the Jesuit
tradition," choose to take classes at the UCA, perform pastoral work
either in San Salvador or out in the countryside, and live in community with each other and with Salvadoran students to whom the
program grants academic scholarships.

Casa Solidaridad is a living embodiment of Jesuit transnationalism, the same Jesuit transnationalism that sent Leo O'Donovan to
meet with President Christiani, Donald Monan to attend the trial
of Colonel Benavides, and Dean Brackley to continue to spend his
life teaching and working at the UCA in El Salvador. These Jesuits,
and hundreds like them, had their perspectives and lives changed
forever when their brothers were killed by a military force that was
armed and paid for by their government. It is fascinating to note
that even the widespread efforts to keep the memory of the martyrs
alive are carried out in ways that are so very characteristic of the Society of Jesus. Jesuits apparently build their symbols and construct
their myths in exactly the same ways in which they structure their
communities and conduct their politics: actively, self-confidently,
transnationally, and *universidadamente*—centered on the meaning
and mission of their educational apostolate.

CHAPTER 3

The People

On Mission from Nicaragua to the United States

Nancy Donovan was already back at the Maryknoll motherhouse in Ossining, New York, when ·I began to visit
her. After thirty years as a missionary in Nicaragua and throughout
Central America, she was living with many other retired Maryknoll
sisters in a sprawling house that feels more like a large college dor-
mitory than a convent. Way too big for Maryknoll's dwindling numbers, it is set on the grounds of a compound whose size and beauty
would put most college campuses to shame. I spent a number of
very pleasant afternoons with Nancy (as she asked to be called),
sitting in one of the house's many reception rooms, eating lunch
in the communal dining room, and going for long walks on the
many paths that wind around the motherhouse. Strolling slowly, we
walked past the publishing offices for Orbis Books and toward the
men's side of the road and the bell yard, where departure ceremo-
nies used to be held each year to mark the sending of hundreds of
intrepid young priests and nuns to spread the Gospel to all corners
of the globe. Nancy's memory was not nearly as clear as either she
or I would have liked it to be during our visits. But throughout our
talks she was always unfailingly gracious and even solicitous. She
was attentive to my appetite, concerned for my safe travel to and
from her home, and always palpably anxious to help in any way that
she could to deepen my understanding of her experiences and of

her Maryknoll Congregation's rapidly and deeply evolving definition of Christian mission.

It is almost impossible to believe that the solicitous woman I
came to know in Ossining was the same Nancy Donovan who had
leapt off a truck in northern Nicaragua in January 1985 so that
she could hike back to her home in San Juan de Limay to warn the
people there that the contras were active in the region once again.
She was so anxious to warn her neighbors that day because she was
convinced that these counterrevolutionary opponents of Nicaragua's Sandinista regime would soon be wreaking havoc on the safety
and security of the innocent civilians who populated the villages
in the Nicaragua-Honduras border region where she lived. It was
even harder for me to picture the rather placid woman I came to
know over lunches in Ossining talking her way out of captivity after
she had been kidnapped by a band of contras as she tried to make
her way on foot back to Limay. Nancy was forced to trek across the
rugged terrain with the contras for the rest of that day. She made
mental notes of their uniforms, their modes of communication,
and their discussion of their future plans; and in the end she negotiated her own release by convincing them that holding her, or
worse yet killing her, would not further their military objectives or
their political cause. Although all of this was hard to picture, over
the course of our conversations at Maryknoll it was easy for me to
develop great respect for this woman who had left her Connecticut
family in 1950 to go to Latin America to save souls, and who had
ended up being consumed by the lives of the people she lived with
and outraged by the US foreign policy that she felt was so antithetical to their interests.

One of Nancy Donovan's favorite stories to tell was of the time,
shortly after her abduction and release, when she testified before
Congress in Washington, DC. More than twenty years later, her be-
mused surprise at her own confidence that day was still palpable
and disarming. When she entered the Maryknoll Congregation,
she never imagined that her work could ever be defined in any way
as "political." She did not imagine that she, as a missionary, would
have testimony to offer about the meaning and ramifications of US

foreign policy. She never in her wildest dreams thought that she would someday sit before the Committee on Foreign Affairs of the US House of Representatives and say:

> As a Christian and as a U.S. citizen, I am deeply pained by the fact that my government has been responsible for arming and training these forces who have systematically caused the deaths of so many unarmed, innocent Nicaraguans for no reasonable purpose. From my personal experience and my faith commitment I need and am obliged to speak out against such an evil, inhumane, and illegal policy. . . . I wish to join my voice and my prayers to that of the U.S. Catholic bishops and that of the churches and faithful across the United States who have protested the U.S. government's support for the Contra forces who kidnap, rape, torture, and kill defenseless civilians, many of whom were my friends and parishioners.[1]

But she did offer that testimony—as a Christian, as a US citizen, and as a missionary. And she offered it because by 1985 she and her Maryknoll colleagues throughout the world were missionaries in a very modern sense of the term. No longer content to staff hospitals and schools (many of which had only catered to what Pedro Arrupe called, in a different context, "the dominant social classes"), and no longer convinced that God willed them to count success by the number of babies they baptized, Nancy and her sisters were by the 1980s committed to a definition of mission that centered on the concept of accompaniment. Animated by their devotion to the poor, the Maryknoll sisters saw their role as being with "the people": sharing the people's privations, their hopes, and their joys, all in the confidence that human solidarity was a value in its own right, and all in the belief that the sisters and the poor could, by sharing their lives with each other, engage in a kind of mutual Christian evangelization. The missioners, as the sisters called themselves, could help the poor claim their rights and their dignity within social systems, economic processes, and political institutions that had marginalized the poor for centuries. And the poor could help the missioners learn experientially about the true humility of poverty and about the profound hope that resides in the heart of every human being, no matter how situated in the world.

For Nancy Donovan, specifically, her mission in the 1980s was to live with the people of Nicaragua as they underwent the upheaval of revolution and the violence of counterrevolution. Her day-to-day work centered on tasks like resettling refugees, supporting and organizing literacy programs for rural women and their children, and helping satisfy the pastoral needs of a remote population that clung to the local church as a source of spiritual solace and physical sustenance. However, Nancy was also accompanying a people whom she understood to be terrorized by a counterrevolutionary army organized, armed, and deployed by her own US government. Anxious to reverse the gains of the Sandinista revolution, the contras were, in Nancy's experience, neither the "freedom fighters" nor the "moral equal of our Founding Fathers" that President Ronald Reagan had claimed they were.[2] Instead she saw the contra forces as a band of terrorists who sabotaged community development projects, intimidated the community as a whole, and, worst of all, regularly assassinated the community's leaders. "We spend much of our time in the cemetery and consoling families"—this is how Nancy described conditions in her town of Limay in northern Nicaragua in a book published in the mid-1980s. "The contras seem to like to go after civilians—anyone who's doing anything to help the town."[3] Given her understanding of mission as accompaniment, Nancy Donovan was not at all surprised that she herself had fallen victim to the contras' tactics when she was captured and held by them. She was living with the people, and she was trying to help them; as Oscar Romero had said of himself and his priests in El Salvador, she fully expected to suffer along with the people of Nicaragua.

But in addition to accompanying the people of Limay and northern Nicaragua through their sufferings and in their hope, Nancy also had another mission—a *reverse mission* to the people of the United States.[4] She felt fully at home in Nicaragua, comfortably rooted in the community to whom she had dedicated her life, and she had not really lived in the United States in decades. But this native of Waterbury, Connecticut, still felt a powerful responsibility to return to the country of her birth and her family so that she could tell the people of the United States what was being done in Nicaragua by their government. Like many other Maryknoll sisters in

Central America, Nancy Donovan believed (perhaps a bit naively) that people in the United States simply must not know what was actually happening, with their tacit support, in unknown places like Limay, Nicaragua. "Americans were buying the bullets that the contras were using to kill the leaders of my village," was how she put it in our interviews.[5] If only she could tell people at home what was really happening—what President Reagan's freedom fighters were actually doing—then she could challenge her fellow Christians to evaluate their government's policies in the light of the religious principles they claimed to profess.

Most of the Maryknoll sisters in Central America were US citizens, and as such they also enjoyed a rootedness in the American national context that could make a real difference for the people with whom they lived. The missioners could testify before Congress, they could be interviewed on television and in newspapers, and they could travel the United States giving witness to what was happening in Central America. Nancy's neighbors in Limay, and the other people with whom the sisters were living throughout the region, could do nothing of the kind, but the sisters could do it for them through the process of reverse mission. Instead of conceptualizing their missionary work as bringing something from the United States to the people of Central America, the sisters saw themselves and their work in almost the opposite terms. A woman like Nancy Donovan, in other words, could be much more than a missionary to the people of San Juan de Limay. She could also be a missionary from the people of Nicaragua back to the United States. She could stake a firm, rooted foot in both contexts. She could bring what she saw as a powerful and painfully obvious truth home from the field, and she could ask her fellow citizens in the United States to take responsibility for what was being done in their name. As she put it with characteristic simplicity, "My country was killing my people."[6] And she knew that she had to try to stop it.

Mission

Nancy Donovan is a member of the Maryknoll Sisters of Saint Dominic, a group of Roman Catholic sisters who, according to their constitution, "[respond] to the invitation of Jesus Christ to go to the ends of the earth to spread the Good News of the Reign of God." "We aspire with others," the constitution says, "to deepen the religious dimension in the lives of all." And with particular emphasis the constitution also says that they have been "invited to journey with the people, especially the poor, the oppressed, and the abandoned." This identification with the poor is not tangential to the Maryknoll mission today; it is the core of it. "We experience God's salvific power," they say, "in our solidarity with the poor, which is not an option, but an imperative of the Gospel of Jesus Christ." This "community," as they call themselves, is in a sense a radical band of women. They form a group of mostly US citizens who are, in their own collective articulation, "willing to risk [their] lives responding in friendship and service to the cause as well as the needs of the poor, the oppressed, and the alienated."[7]

The sisters of Maryknoll did not start with such a mission in mind, however. In fact, when the sisters first gathered in Ossining in 1911, they were not yet sisters at all. They were instead "the secretaries," a group of clerical assistants to the men who were in the process of founding the Catholic Missionary Society of America. Two priests, James Walsh and Thomas Price, began what quickly came to be known as the Maryknoll society to fill what they saw as an embarrassing gap in American ecclesiastical structures at the turn of the twentieth century. Since the United States was no longer classified by the Vatican as "mission territory," it was high time for the United States to do its part in evangelizing the rest of the world. Mollie Rogers, now the venerated foundress of the Maryknoll sisters, was then the leader of a small group of pious women who were recruited by Walsh to come to Ossining to help him in the laborious task of establishing a priestly society that would send missionaries—*male* missionaries—to China.

The secretaries, as they were then known, performed under Mollie's leadership the "women's work" of the new Maryknoll order. They cooked for the men, they cleaned for the men, and they performed the clerical duties for the men that their designation implied. Among the most important and portentous of the latter, however, were the complex tasks the secretaries performed in producing and distributing Maryknoll's first periodical, *The Field Afar*. This magazine, whose name would later be changed to *Maryknoll*, publicized, and in truth romanticized, the exploits of the new missionary society for the purposes of raising its profile, funding its activities, and enticing new recruits to its adventures. Maryknoll heroes like Francis X. Ford, the eventually martyred bishop of "Red China," were first introduced to a captivated reading audience across American Catholicism in the pages of *The Field Afar*.

It is important to remember, so far removed in time, that James Walsh, Mollie Rogers, and their colleagues—both in "the field afar" and in Ossining—were devoted and devout members of a Church that in that era taught that there was no eternal salvation outside the confines of their own Roman Catholicism. They believed, as a matter of literal truth, that through their missionary work they were saving pagan souls, opening the gates of heaven to human beings who would otherwise languish in eternal darkness (or worse) simply because of the accidental misfortune of being born in a "heathen land." To the pioneering generation of Maryknoll, male and female alike, their missionary endeavors were the first necessary step to the work of God on earth. All other interests and priorities, no matter how noble, were for them secondary to the fundamental task of preaching the Gospel in new lands and baptizing new Catholics for the Lord.

The work of the secretaries was a crucial part of all of this, of course, but Rogers and the original small group of women she led were not satisfied. They wanted to do much more than Walsh envisioned them doing in Ossining. Almost from the very beginning the secretaries wanted to serve in the foreign missions themselves. A necessary step in that process was for them to be recognized formally as a religious congregation, but that was not an easy process. The growing community of women in Ossining went through a number of frustrating fits and starts as they moved forward along their desired path to canonical recognition and finally to assignment in the missions. They evolved from "the secretaries" to self-styled "Teresians" (after the heroic example of Saint Teresa of Avila), through an unsuccessful apprenticeship with the Franciscans, until finally they were formally recognized by the Vatican (or "founded") in 1920 as the Foreign Mission Sisters of Saint Dominic.[8]

Even once they had donned their distinctive grey habits and set sail for China, however, the sisters' work was still intended to support the men who had preceded them from Ossining to mission. Dana Robert used the term "auxiliary" to capture the early work of the Maryknoll women and to place their congregation's founding in the broader context of the subservient position of women religious in relation to "the prerogatives of the male hierarchy and men's missionary orders."[9] These atmospherics of dependency were one of the defining features of the sisters' early experience in mission. And this atmosphere was reinforced by the hero-making literature that was at that time creating a powerful mythology around the *Adventures of Men of Maryknoll,* as a 1957 book was later titled, with a not incidental emphasis on the word "men."[10]

Without a doubt, this auxiliary status greatly restricted the scope of the sisters' activities once they actually reached the "ends of the earth" and began to win souls for the Church. But it soon became apparent, to the sisters and more importantly to "their" priests, that women religious could do things and go places that the men could not. The sisters were expected to play traditionally female roles as teachers and nurses in schools and hospitals run exclusively by priests. But the men and women of Maryknoll soon learned that only female Westerners were welcome to visit the homes of the Chinese people, whom all of the Maryknoll missionaries were hoping to evangelize.

A reciprocal dynamic was at work here as well, by the way: a dynamic that marked the sisters as female missionaries in a powerful way from practically the very beginning. Unlike their male colleagues, many of the Maryknoll women found themselves drawn powerfully to defining at least part of their particular mission as defending and articulating the dignity of Chinese women *as women.* In the words of Penny Lernoux, whose *Hearts on Fire* is the leading history of the Maryknoll women, many of the sisters hoped to "save Chinese babies, especially girls, who were routinely abandoned in ditches and on the streets."[11] But in time that sensitivity to and emphasis on the female experience of the Chinese also found its way into the sisters' testimony to the belief in the equal value of female life. Women's dignity was, according to Lernoux, a keynote for the female Maryknoll missionaries right from the very beginning.

This found its direct practical application in the courageous and innovative decision by Francis X. Ford, the Maryknoll bishop in China, to assign "his" sisters, through the so-called Kaying experiment, to go out "two by two" to live, work, and evangelize among the people in the remotest areas of rural China. In this early portent of their modern commitment to accompaniment, the sisters in China also begin to emphasize the degree to which their mission was being lived out as a mission to the poor. Lernoux again: "Long before the 1960s when religious orders made a preferential option for the poor, the Maryknoll sisters were living it. . . . Evangelization was to become linked to a large extent with identification with the poor."[12]

Developments like the commitment to Ford's Kaying experiment in China led the Maryknoll sisters at long last to move beyond the role of auxiliaries to the men and into the direct work of evangelization and mission. The energetic daughters of American Catholicism who fanned out across China, Korea, the Philippines, and later Bolivia, Peru, and then all of Latin America were still mostly tied in their day-to-day work to institutions and to traditional women's work in education and health care. They were in many ways the paradigmatic examples of female missionaries as they staffed their orphanages in China, their schools in Peru, and their hospital in Tanzania. But they were also fulfilling the founding dream of Mollie Rogers (now known by her religious name, Mother Mary Joseph) of "going out to the outermost parts of the Earth . . . to bring His name to those who do not know Him."[13] They were going out not as assistants to priests or auxiliaries to men, but in their own right as women and as missioners. And it is worth noting that in so doing they were also creating their own mythical aura to match that of the Maryknoll men. The martyrdom tales of Francis Ford and Patrick Byrne in China were in time told alongside the compelling ordeal of Sister Trinita and Sister Brigita at the hands of their Japanese captors in the Philippines.[14] Movies like *The Bamboo Curtain* and the swashbuckling literary stylings of Sister Maria del Rey helped define the Maryknoll mission in female terms for a whole generation of viewers and readers.[15] As a result, the sisters' numbers soared; the huge motherhouse was built in Ossining; the Maryknoll women were, in a way, a kind of foreign legion of female American Catholicism triumphant.

New Habits

The institutional milieu that nurtured and shaped this growth and mission was relatively short-lived. The young women who headed to Ossining in these years to give their lives to God and the missions had no idea how profoundly their understanding of that mission would change over the life of their service. The core of Mollie Rogers's founding mission would remain intact throughout. But so much of what the sisters did—and just as importantly, so much of how they thought about what they did—was radically transformed by the reforms of the Second Vatican Council and by the social revolutions that hit America and American Catholicism in the 1960s and 1970s. It might even be fair to say that the seismic shifts that convulsed Roman Catholicism in the United States and throughout the world in those days had their deepest effect on women in religious life in general, and on Maryknollers and other female missioners in particular. In a thoroughgoing transformation that was breathtaking in retrospect, one that Marie Augusta Neal has defined as the path "from nuns to sisters," these women left the cloister and convent (literally and figuratively), exchanged their habits for civilian clothes, and immersed themselves in the lives, communities, and, significantly, the sufferings of the poor people whom they felt called to accompany and serve.[16]

When the Second Vatican Council, in its *Pastoral Constitution on the Church in the Modern World*, said that the joys, hopes, and griefs of the world's people are also the joys, hopes, and griefs of the Catholic Church, this was pretty much a direct invitation for groups like the Maryknoll sisters to reconceptualize their definition of mission and rededicate themselves to active service. This message was revolutionary for all of American Catholicism, of course. Having spent the preceding century painstakingly constructing a distinctive Catholic subculture and parochial Catholic institutions to insulate a beleaguered Church from a hostile environment, American Catholics were now instructed in the 1960s by the universal Church's most authoritative teaching documents "to be open to the world, to the duty of scrutinizing the signs of the times, and of interpreting them in the light of the gospel."[17] That would prove to be a complex charge, and in truth the suburban Church in the United States is still struggling with how to be a part of such an affluent and comfortable society while remaining critical of that society's economic, political, and social values. But for the Maryknoll women living and working in far-flung missions in the 1960s and 1970s, the "signs of the times" were glaringly obvious, and what was needed in terms of "interpreting them in the light of the gospel" was really not that complicated.

The predominant sign of the times in the mid-twentieth century was that the modern systems of economic distribution, political organization, and social hierarchy were deeply damaging to the interests of the world's poorest peoples. And the lesson of the Gospel that just as obviously needed to be applied was that something had to be done about it. Something had to be done in response to that damage—even if that something was a simple commitment to live with the poor, honor their dignity, and share in their joy, grief, and, most importantly, hope for a better future.

Not at all coincidentally, the challenges of Vatican II were reinforced in the experience of many Maryknoll sisters by the analysis—and the justifications, if you will—of what came to be called liberation theology. This was a very complex time in Catholic history, and any attempt to order it in a clear sequence opens up the possibility and danger of confusion and anachronism. But when Maryknoll was driven out of Asia by Japanese militarism and Chinese communism, the priests and sisters shifted a significant portion of their operations to Bolivia, then Peru, and in time to all of Latin America. There they came into contact with local theologians who were beginning to write of Jesus Christ as liberator and of the Catholic Church's "preferential option for the poor." Dana Robert put it well: "The changing role of the sisters merged with the nascent theology of liberation to propel the sisters towards closer life with the poor."[18]

Liberation theology ran into some ecclesial trouble later on. The universal Church came under the leadership of a Polish pope who had his own nationally idiosyncratic understandings of industrial relations, the responsibilities of capital, and the definition of liberation in Christ. But for many Maryknoll sisters, the central insights of the new school of theology rang decidedly legitimate. The poor were not suffering because of their own lassitude, or because of impersonal forces of nature, or because of God's will. The poor were suffering because of economic, political, and social structures that directly benefited the rich (or at least the richer) at the expense of the poor (and especially the poorer). The sisters did not set out to "afflict the comfortable" (as the saying put it at that time). But they certainly did believe that it was the role of their Catholic Church to comfort the afflicted. And if that meant putting their Church and themselves in conflict with land owners, military leaders, local political elites, and US foreign policy, then so be it.

For the Society of Jesus, as we saw in chapter 2, the transformation of their central commitment to one of "service of faith in the promotion of justice" came at their Thirty-Second General Congregation in 1974. For the Maryknoll Sisters of Saint Dominic, a similar process took place over the course of a series of general assemblies and special meetings between 1964 and 1970. These meetings charted a new course for the Maryknoll Congregation that proved, in the words of Penny Lernoux, to be "the permanent harbinger of the Maryknollers' future."[19] The general assembly of 1964 met in the middle of the Second Vatican Council (1962–65) and focused especially on the specific ways in which Maryknoll could and should respond to what the Italians called the *aggiornamento*, or opening, set in motion by Pope John XXIII. For Maryknollers, *aggiornamento* meant, in a word, accompaniment. It meant a responsibility as missionaries to serve the poor in order to play a role in liberating the poor from oppression.

The most significant and self-defining session of all for the Maryknoll sisters, however, was a special meeting called in 1968, where the sisters set out four goals of their reformulated mission in a document called *Mission Challenges*. These four goals were as follows:

1. to foster fraternal unity among cultures
2. to help local church communities develop in strength and cohesion
3. to build the universal Catholic Church through its unity as "the people of God"
4. to help local churches to develop their own missionary dynamic, and to fulfill their own intrinsic mission vocation

A document released by the subsequent general assembly in 1970 called "Searching and Sharing" ratified these four goals in a clear and legal formulation as the purposes and commitments of Maryknoll sisters all over the world. At the same meeting, the sisters also took the symbolic democratizing step of changing the title of their leader from "mother general" to "president." And it was one of the early presidents, Melinda Roper, who defined mission in these ringing terms: "My understanding of our mission today is to bring consistently and perserveringly the perspectives and causes of the poor, oppressed and repressed of our world into all discussions of life in our society, and to do so in the spirit of the Gospel."[20]

More prosaically, but also far more personally, Bernice Kita, serving in Guatemala during the violent upheavals that tore up that country during the 1980s, wrote that she and her Maryknoll sisters understood their work through what she called "the post–Vatican II conception of the missionary who came to serve and to learn with the people." Kita wrote to her own mother at one point, advising that "if people ever ask what your daughter does for a living, tell them that she's present." "I am growing in awareness," she wrote, "that my presence here is my main contribution to the people."[21] Another Maryknoll sister, Ita Ford, a niece of the legendary Maryknoll bishop and martyr Francis Ford of China, would herself, as we will see shortly, become a martyr to the Maryknoll mission and to the "perspectives and causes of the poor." A couple of years before her death, reflecting on her understanding of her mission in Latin America, Ford had asked: "Am I willing to suffer with the people here, the suffering of the powerless, the feeling impotent? Can I say to my neighbors—I have no solutions to the situation; I don't know the answers, but I will walk with you, search with you, be with you."[22]

Encountering Politics

The Maryknoll sisters describe themselves as being devoted to "contemplation in action," a phrase similar to the one the Jesuits use to describe themselves.[23] And emphasizing, in these years surrounding the Second Vatican Council, the responsibility to act versus the value of contemplation, the sisters headed out two by two, four by four, once in a while ten by ten, to live out their mission among the people without the formal protection and sanctuary of a convent (much less a cloister) or the obvious distinctiveness of a religious habit. Unlike the Jesuits, however, this mission was no longer lived out mostly through the founding and staffing of institutions. The sisters did still run schools, and they also ran and staffed hospitals, clinics, refugee centers, farming cooperatives, and a large variety of apostolates and missions. But the institutions were no longer the point in and of themselves. The institutions were in large part methods for getting closest to the people who were most in need. As one Maryknoll sister in El Salvador put it to me in describing her work, the sisters went out to find poor people in great need . . . and then they moved in next door to them.[24]

These were not "political" decisions in the narrow, formal sense of the term. Most of these women, after all, had come to Maryknoll for traditional reasons, committed in the words of the Congregation's first constitution to "being sent to pagans" and "heathen lands" for "personal sanctification," seeking to convert others to Christianity or, failing that, to baptize their abandoned babies.[25] Peggy Healy, one of the sisters who would later find herself deeply involved in political processes, went to great lengths to emphasize in an interview with me that there was absolutely, positively nothing political either about her decision to join Maryknoll or about her early work as a nurse in Nicaragua when she was first sent into mission. Speaking of her family on Long Island and of her decision to join Maryknoll and work in Nicaragua, Healy said, "We were not a political family. I hadn't given politics a single thought. . . . I was going down there to be a nurse. There was no politics for us in it at the time."[26]

I believe her. I do not doubt at all that the sisters went into mission without either realizing or desiring the political ramifications of what they did and with whom they identified. But regardless of their intentions or their expectations, it became obvious that to live with the poor in solidarity, and to share in the poor's privations and insecurities along with the poor's joys and hopes, was to experience firsthand what liberation theologians and others referred to as the sinful structures of modern political economies. Moreover, to identify so closely in the 1970s with the poor in Central America—Healy readily called her neighbors in Nicaragua "my people," "my family," and "people you would happily die for"[27]—and with their basic demands for water, for decent education, and most controversially for land—was to offer public support to one side (the losing side, it must be said) in a series of sharp conflicts between the "have almost everythings" and the "have practically nothings." In time there was no getting around that recognition for the sisters. And in time there was no sense denying that such an identification was, in some very important ways, *political.* Mohammed Ahrari wrote of the levels of connectedness that tie ethnic populations to each other across national borders as the key to the political mobilizations that define ethnic lobbies. Obviously these Maryknoll sisters did not share ethnic identity with the people they lived with in Central America. But they nevertheless shared a level of communal identification and solidarity with people that they "would happily die for" that motivated, animated, and, in their own eyes at least, validated all of the sisters' political activism.

These conflicts in Central America—in Guatemala, Nicaragua, and El Salvador—were escalating into violent full-blown revolutionary civil wars exactly during those years when the Second Vatican Council was encouraging the sisters to redefine their mission. As a result the Maryknoll sisters, like the Jesuits at the UCA in San Salvador, found themselves in the crosshairs of brutal counterrevolutionary countermeasures being taken by local military and paramilitary forces who were trained, funded, and fully supported by the government of the United States of America. Unlike Ignacio Ellacuría and his colleagues at the UCA, however, people like Nancy Donovan, Peggy Healy, Bernice Kita, and Ita Ford were themselves US citizens. For them the conflict between US policy and their religious, social, and political commitments was felt at a much more personal level. For them, their dual identity (to again introduce a loaded term) as Catholic missioners and US citizens—their deep rootedness in both contexts—conferred on them very particular responsibilities.

In truth the position in which the Maryknoll sisters found themselves by the early 1980s required (or, better said, reflected) a whole new relationship between the Maryknoll mission and US foreign policy. An occasional ambivalence had cropped up in that relationship from time to time across Maryknoll history. But by and large the relationship between Maryknoll mission and US foreign policy was conceived by the missioners, and by outside observers, as one of presumed agreement, mutual support, and natural reinforcement. The first mission field for the Maryknoll fathers had been China, after all; and given the unquestioned assumptions of that period in US political history, it was no surprise that those fathers sympathized with the nationalist cause in its battle with Mao's communist revolution. In the pages of *The Field Afar*, the "evil Reds" were presented as every bit as much the enemies of the Maryknoll Congregation (and the Catholic Church) as they were of the United States of America. Indeed no distinction was even made between the two, as a Maryknoll man like Francis Ford felt that it was part of his mission to report on "Communist troop movements, economic conditions, communication and transportation facilities in his area."[28] The communists, when they found such incriminating evidence in Ford's files, declared Maryknoll to be "the biggest spy ring in China."[29] The Maryknoll fathers may have denied the specific charge of spying. But they did not bother to deny the pervasive effects of their sympathies.

This identification of America's policy aims with Maryknoll's religious mission was part of a much broader trend in American Catholicism at that time. The Catholic hierarchy, and what was then known as the Catholic lobby, exuded what Dorothy Dohen has termed a "superpatriotic" support of American foreign policy in general, and the anticommunist crusade in particular.[30] In the first place, American Catholic leaders, both clerical and lay, really did see a profound connection between their faith and their patriotism, between their cross and their flag. Communism was "Godless communism," and its advance in places like China, Korea, and Vietnam was widely viewed in Catholic circles as a satanic evil, literally.

There was a second reason for Catholic superpatriotism, however, and that second reason was based on more practical considerations. The American Catholic population was at the middle of the twentieth century still largely an immigrant population that was still subject to nativist prejudice and still challenged to defend its dual loyalty to Church and to nation. Paul Blanshard's *American Freedom and Catholic Power* was published in 1950, and it crystallized, though in decidedly overheated terms, a fairly pervasive sense within American Protestantism that first- and second-generation American Catholics were untrustworthy in terms of their devotion and support for their adopted country.[31] What better way was there to debunk such canards than with unquestioning support for American foreign policy? A central Catholic riposte to anti-Catholicism, then, was the adoption of a "more patriotic than thou" ethos. By identifying the Catholic cause with the anticommunist one, in other words, Catholic leaders were not only fighting a common enemy; they were also establishing the patriotic bona fides of a (still) beleaguered American Catholic population.

No one embodied this dynamic more clearly and completely than Francis Spellman. As the cardinal archbishop of New York and also the Catholic vicar of the US armed forces, Spellman allowed not a sliver of room between himself and official anticommunist rhetoric, policies, or war. "My country, may it always be right," he said at the height of the Vietnam War, "but right or wrong, my country."[32] It was no surprise, then, that Spellman took on with special relish an unofficial role as the "protector of Maryknoll," the best-known group of his Catholic countrymen and countrywomen serving in foreign mission. He spoke out often in support of the Maryknollers and their work abroad. He supported the publication of turgid volumes like *Nun in Red China*.[33] And when he needed a place to park Ngo Dinh Diem, before Diem could safely return to South Vietnam as its Catholic, anticommunist leader, Spellman chose, naturally enough, a Maryknoll seminary as the future Vietnamese president's American sanctuary. In time Spellman's reflexive sanctification of US aims in Vietnam would be joined, if not replaced, in the public's consciousness by the image of priests and nuns marching against the Vietnam War and burning draft records with homemade napalm. Indeed Francis Spellman would eventually become an institutional embarrassment for many American Catholics, a kind of anachronistic old uncle who insisted on the dictates of superpatriotism long after it remained either useful or sensible. But for a period of several decades encompassing World War II and the height of the Cold War, Spellman's uncritical jingoism spoke for a central strain in American Catholicism—praise the Lord and pass the ammunition.

To be sure, Maryknoll sisters were neither as ham-handed nor as overtly political as either Francis Spellman or Francis Ford were. But they nevertheless in the main asserted the very close identification of the romanticized tales of "nuns in Red China" with American foreign policy. This connection had actually been deeply established during the Second World War through the popularization of the horrific treatment endured by Maryknoll sisters in Japanese prison camps in the Philippines. For those sisters, and their legions of supporters in Catholic parishes and schools across America, there simply was no difference between the spiritual struggles being fought by missionaries in Asia and the military struggles being fought by "our boys" in the same locales. "We go where the U.S. Government goes," the sisters said as they "flew with the eagle" all over Asia, and then all over the world.[34] Amazingly, given subsequent developments, "flying with the eagle" was much more than a metaphor for the US patriotism felt so strongly by the missionaries; Maryknoll sisters were actually transported to China in this period on US military aircraft.[35]

A Central American corollary to this political dynamic was symbolized by a Christmas dinner party that a group of Maryknoll sisters attended in 1944 with Anastasio Somoza, the United States–backed dictator of Nicaragua.[36] By their own later accounts, these sisters never thought to question their association with a figure who would prove in the long run to be so controversial, so brutal, and so antithetical to Maryknoll's work among the Nicaraguan poor. They never considered, really, that their reflexive approbation of US policy and US agents was in its own way a form of political expression. Surely they could scarcely imagine at the time that they and their successors would in a matter of a few short decades be publicly opposing the regime of Somoza's son, or that some of them would be testifying before the US Congress in support of the revolutionary movement that would eventually drive the Somoza regime from power. The sisters who met and dined with the dictator in the 1940s were in Nicaragua to do the pastoral work of teaching in Catholic schools and nursing in Catholic hospitals. As they saw it at the time, there was absolutely nothing political about them or about their mission—until, that is, they began to wonder what values and structures they and their work were actually supporting. Until they decided through their Vatican II transformation to read the signs of the times, and apply the lessons of the Gospel to them. Until, in short, they began to wonder whose side they were on.

This transformation took place for most of the sisters very gradually, imperceptibly even. I have already described the process in terms of the wordings of the Maryknoll constitutions. But in the field, for the actual women living and working in mission, the shift to a position of what can fairly be called oppositional activism grew organically as a function of their accompaniment and identification with what they all came to call "the people." Nancy Donovan, for example, never imagined when she left her family for Ossining that she would one day be given a certificate as an honorary member of the Sandinista National Liberation Front of Nicaragua. She was not much interested in theoretical debates about political organization and/or economic distribution. But in her direct experience, in her own village, and with her own neighbors, the Sandinistas were on the side of the people, and that was enough for her.

Peggy Healy described in an interview with me how the political dynamics developed and played out in her own *barrio* in Nicaragua in the 1970s. "The reality was," she told me, "that [we] were being put in a place where lines were being drawn. And as the revolutionary movements got stronger, so did the repression."[37] For Healy and her immediate colleagues, the seminal event was a conflict with a local water company over access to water and unfair pricing mechanisms related to that access. That water fight, as she calls it, ignited simmering tensions in her village, and the conflict quickly escalated through the arrest of local leaders and organizers and on to open conflict with the government and its armed enforcers. "We would have tugs of war," Healy recalled, "with the National Guard over people they were trying to take. . . . It got worse and worse, and then we started to see the red and black flags [of the Sandinista Front]."[38]

The relationship between Maryknoll and the revolutionary movements in this period is still shrouded in political controversy. With more than a hint of patronization, the sisters were dismissed as naive at best and actively subversive at worst. Criticisms of the sisters' politicization of their mission (and of the Gospel) continues to this day, and I have sensed a palpable defensiveness on the part of these women when they discuss their activities in that period. They take great pains to try to convince listeners (like me) that they were not "political," or at least that they had not set out to participate in politics. Political participation came and found them, they argue, in the form of oppression of the people they felt called to serve. My own intention here, of course, is neither to judge nor characterize the sisters' commitments of thirty years ago. Rather, it is my intention to highlight the political significance of the simple fact that for many energetic and articulate American Catholic women in the late 1970s and early 1980s, the concepts of "my country," on the one hand, and "my people," on the other, had come to diverge rather dramatically.

The US Marines, which an earlier generation of Maryknollers had naturally identified as "the boys"—especially when those boys rescued the sisters from the Los Banos prison camp during World War II—were now in a troubling sense a potential enemy, or at least a potential enemy to people with whom the sisters had become extremely close. In that context it was *los muchachos* of the revolutionary movements who were identified, in the minds of some Maryknoll missioners, with the interests and aspirations of "the people." The political context was exceedingly complex in those days, and the ideological alliances are still difficult to disentangle even all these years later. But two things were perfectly clear and easily named. First, by binding themselves so closely to the people, the missioners were placing themselves in opposition to an American foreign policy that was still closely associated with the very structures that the people were struggling against. Second, in accompanying the Central American people in their struggle, the Maryknoll sisters were placing themselves, knowingly and willingly, in mortal danger. Indeed intimidation and threats became common. And in December 1980, just nine months after the assassination of Oscar Romero, and nine years before the carnage at the UCA, four female missioners from the United States, including two Maryknoll sisters, were murdered in El Salvador.

Ita and Maura

The names Ita Ford and Maura Clarke are, if possible, even more closely identified with the Maryknoll mission to the people of Central America than Rutilio Grande and Ignacio Ellacuría are with the Jesuits' mission. Joining Oscar Romero in the pantheon of modern martyrs, Ita and Maura, as they are always called (along with their non-Maryknoll colleagues Dorothy Kazel and Jean Donovan) are thought by many to be modern-day saints. They have not yet been canonized as saints by the Vatican (neither has Romero, for that matter), but they have been idealized and sacralized by millions since their murders in December 1980. The first and most obvious reason for this status is the public and brutal nature of their deaths. Their van was commandeered by a group of out-of-uniform soldiers on the road leading from the airport in San Salvador and was directed onto a small side road, where they were raped, shot, and haphazardly buried in a shallow grave. For a certain segment of the Catholic population in the United States, the famous photo of Maryknoll nuns kneeling in prayer as their sisters were pulled from that makeshift grave is iconic and galvanizing.

But the second reason Ita and Maura are so very important to the Maryknoll community is that the two sisters were killed precisely because they were carrying out the clearly defined mission of the Congregation. As young women, Ita Ford and Maura Clarke had joined a very different Maryknoll Congregation than the one they were representing in El Salvador by 1980. They had originally been fairly typical of the suburban girls who had headed off to Ossining to win souls for Christ, but they had evolved along with their community and had embraced with passion and courage the modern mission of accompaniment and service. Maura Clarke had spent many years teaching school in Nicaragua and had brought her quiet resolve to El Salvador only a few short months before the killings. Ita Ford, for her part, had cut a fairly unusual path through her years in Maryknoll, joining as a teenager, leaving due to illness, and finding her way back in her twenties. She had lived through the tumult in Chile after the coup in 1973 that toppled Salvador Allende and installed a military government, and she too was a relative newcomer to El Salvador.

Both women had embodied the depth of the Maryknoll commitment to Central America by volunteering to go to El Salvador in the first place. El Salvador was a very violent and dangerous place in 1980. But Ita and Maura went anyway for three interrelated reasons: to express their solidarity with the Maryknoll sisters who were already working there; to have the chance to be swept up in the prophetic tide unleashed by Oscar Romero; and to serve where their discernment, and their superiors back in New York, believed that the needs of the people were most dire.

Their work in El Salvador centered on responding to the physical and pastoral needs of persons displaced by the political violence that was then engulfing the country. As Maryknoll sisters almost always insist, regardless of the context, the women in El Salvador did not consider their work political in the usual sense of that word. But in combining attentiveness to the needs of the displaced with an articulation of the rights of the dispossessed, the sisters were engaged in work that the military and political leaders of the country classified as political, and indeed subversive. And given the brutal practices of the Salvadoran regime at the time, the sisters suffered, as the title of a book about them describes it, "the same fate as the poor."[39]

The killing of the four churchwomen in El Salvador became a cause célèbre in the United States immediately. For one thing, the timing of the event played an important role in how it was covered in the press. Ronald Reagan had defeated President Jimmy Carter in the presidential election just a month before, and the president-elect was in the process of assembling his foreign policy team for the new administration. The revolutionary movements in Central America had been an important foreign policy issue during the campaign, with Reagan denouncing Carter's "loss of Nicaragua" and pledging that the United States would take a much more aggressive posture in defense of the next "domino," El Salvador. Throwing gas on the political fire, Jeane Kirkpatrick, Reagan's choice to be US ambassador to the United Nations, said that the women were "not just nuns, they were political activists."[40] And in a statement that earned him the enduring disdain of many Catholics, the new secretary of state, Alexander Haig, claimed in January 1981 that the women had attempted to run a roadblock and had subsequently been killed during an "exchange of fire."[41] For some people the murders were an indication of how deeply and naively some of these American women had waded into the leftist politics of Central America. They did not quite deserve their fate, of course, but they had played with political fire—and they had gotten burned by politics. For others the lessons were just the opposite. Focusing on the innocent-looking faces that smiled out from the suddenly ubiquitous pictures of the four women, what might be called the progressive wing of US Catholicism adopted Ita, Maura, Dorothy, and Jean as patron saints of a movement designed to highlight the injustices wrought by US foreign policy in Central America.

For the Maryknoll Congregation itself, the deaths, in the words of Peggy Healy, "profoundly changed everyone . . . from the soul on outward."[42] She meant by this two things. The first is that the murder of Ita Ford and Maura Clarke demonstrated to all of the sisters in a very concrete way who they were, what they were doing, and what their mission could actually lead to in the political tinderbox of Central America in the 1980s. It was one thing to commit oneself to accompanying the poor as they faced their problems and their fate. It was another thing to realize viscerally that commitment and accompaniment could lead to rape and murder on a back road in El Salvador. Moreover, like the Jesuits would do a long decade later, the Maryknoll sisters in 1980 were forced to face the very challenging fact that dark political forces, supported by their own US government, had killed two of their own. I do not intend any disrespect to the Jesuits, nor to their wholly understandable sense of personal grievance and outrage, when I point out, however, that the Maryknoll sisters seemed to operate under a different and more expansive definition of exactly who it was that counted as "ours." Of course the sisters felt personal grief at the loss of their friends, and of course they passionately desired that the perpetrators of the crime be brought to justice. But their overwhelming sense of solidarity and even identity with the Salvadoran people, and their conception of themselves as missionaries, led them immediately and enduringly to embed their murdered sisters in the wider "ours" of the Salvadoran poor. Maryknoll's President Melinda Roper, on the day that the murders were confirmed, said, "For some fifty years, the Salvadoran people have been struggling for freedom under military rule. Disappearances and killings are nothing new to this wartorn country but have instead increasingly become the order of the day. It is estimated that nine thousand people have been killed in the last year alone, eighty percent of these deaths attributed to paramilitary groups covertly backed by the government."[43]

The other meaning of Healy's report of a profound change in Maryknoll was that, as she put it to me, the deaths of Ita and Maura "also put Maryknoll in a huge place in the media world."[44] Needless to say, this was a form of notoriety that none of the sisters would have sought. But it was notoriety nonetheless, and the sisters became the focus of not only the media's attention, but also the attention of advocacy groups and politicians who, at that time, were growing more and more interested in learning about what was actually happening in places like El Salvador and Nicaragua. The Reagan administration was offering one narrative: Central America was a vital region for the United States. We were supporting imperfect governments there, to be sure, but those governments were our crucial allies against communist subversion, inspired by Moscow and directed through Cuba; these revolutionary movements posed a direct threat to US interests, and even to US national security; and if we did not support the Salvadoran government, and later the con-tras in Nicaragua, then the United States was going to have a much larger and much more dangerous communist menace on its hands in its very own "backyard."

There was, of course, another narrative available for describing what was happening in Central America at that time. This alter-native rejected the idea of a global communist conspiracy and re-fused to see El Salvador and Nicaragua and Guatemala as dominoes poised between the past of Cuba and the future of Miami Beach. This alternative emphasized the brutality of the local regimes and expressed outrage at US support for governments who denied land, justice, and dignity to such large percentages of their own popula-tions. It was articulated by groups like the Washington Office on Latin America (WOLA) and Witness for Peace, and it grew in reso-nance on the left wing of American politics throughout the 1970s and 1980s.

The rape and murder of the churchwomen in El Salvador opened up a much larger space in which that alternative narrative could be heard with credibility in churches, community organiza-tions, and even the halls of power in Washington, DC. Giving voice to that narrative, giving voice to the voiceless of Central America, became a central aspect of the mission of the Maryknoll missioners. The sisters actually lived in Central America. Many of them were convinced that the descriptions and accounts of Reagan officials were false and pernicious. So they took it upon themselves to try to articulate an alternative, to try to evangelize US citizens about what the sisters saw as the actual political and social reality in America's "backyard."

Reverse Mission

This kind of reverse mission has a long history in the Maryknoll experience. As I said earlier, an important motivation for the pub-lication of *The Field Afar* and later *Maryknoll* magazines was to educate Catholic readers not only about what the missioners were doing, but also about why they were doing it and where they were doing it. The tenor of the magazine changed along with the focus of the Maryknoll mission, but the Congregation always had as part of its purpose the idea of sensitizing Catholics in the United States to conditions and imperatives in places far, far away from the experience of most US citizens. This idea of evangelizing the complacent, if you will, was also part of the stewardship work that Maryknoll sisters and fathers would periodically perform when they came home from the field.

Every few years members of the Congregation would return from their mission sites to Ossining to reconnect with the larger community, staff the administrative offices of the motherhouse, and travel to parishes and community groups to recount their experiences and raise money to support their work abroad. Several generations of US Catholics can recall special Sunday Masses when the "good father" or the "good sister" would regale the congregation with tales from their work "in the missions" and ask for special monetary contributions to help the missioners in their work. Again, as the mission evolved so did the presentations. The sermons, speeches, and presentations became less akin to exotic travelogues, and more devoted to bearing witness to the suffering of "the people" and to the complicity of the US government—and of those listening in the pews—in that suffering.

Maura Clarke herself had spoken a few years before her death in El Salvador, addressing both the importance of this stewardship mission and the frustrations inherent in it. She had rotated back to the United States from Nicaragua in the fall of 1976 to perform what she and the other sisters called "mission education work" in Catholic parishes and schools. Those years in the late 1970s were crucial years in the history of Nicaragua, culminating in the Sandinista victory in 1979. Clarke chafed against the limitations of her work in the United States during those years, and she longed to be back with "her people" in Nicaragua. But following her superior's orders obediently, she did what she could from the United States for her people in Nicaragua by actively participating in World Awareness Programs, workshops designed to educate US citizens about what was happening abroad. Reticent as she was, she even spoke at a rally protesting US policy in support of the Somoza regime "and urged those present to appeal to President Carter and Congress to recognize the just struggle of the Nicaraguan people, to support democratic movements rather than 'friendly dictatorships,' and to work to develop more equitable relationships among nations."[45] She implored her colleagues in Nicaragua to demand her return from the states so that she could rejoin them in service in the field. But they demurred. What she was doing in the United States was seen by all of the sisters as crucial work in support of their mission.

Sometimes both the reverse mission and the related political advocacy have had a much sharper edge. Many Americans, Catholic Americans in particular, are familiar with the so-called Catonsville Nine. They were a group of anti-Vietnam War protesters, led by two priests, Daniel Berrigan and his brother Philip Berrigan, who entered a draft board office in Catonsville, Maryland, in 1968. They seized draft records stored there and then burned them in the parking lot with homemade napalm. The action was part of a larger Catholic antiwar movement at the time, and it was memorialized in Daniel Berrigan's play *The Trial of the Catonsville Nine*.[46] I imagine, however, that very few Americans, Catholic or otherwise, knew then or remember today that the Catonsville Nine also included Thomas Melville, a former Maryknoll priest, and his wife, Marjorie Melville, a former Maryknoll sister. The Melvilles were in Maryland that day not only, or even not mostly, to protest the war in Vietnam but also and mainly in the hope of publicly drawing a connection between the American war in Vietnam and American complicity in the repression of the poor in Guatemala.

The Melvilles remain to this day rather controversial figures within the wider Maryknoll community. They met and subsequently fell in love when they were both serving as missioners in the political cauldron that was Guatemala in the 1960s. They bonded over a shared impatience with the pace of social change in Guatemala and through a life-changing frustration at the limits of traditional pastoral and missionary work. Tom Melville, then a priest, grew increasingly outraged at the brutality his rural parishioners were enduring at the hands of the Guatemalan military; and then Maryknoll sister Marjorie Bradford grew increasingly frustrated at the constraints of her work educating the children of the elite in

Guatemala City. There was nothing unusual about their impatience; many Maryknollers felt similar frustrations. But what was unusual was that both of them, unlike other Maryknoll missioners then and since, crossed a clear line of political demarcation when they decided to link their pastoral work directly with the violent revolutionary efforts of antigovernment guerillas. In what became known within the Maryknoll community as the "Melville incident," the couple decided to take up arms in the struggle against the Guatemalan regime. The controversy lay more in the decision itself rather than in any subsequent fighting, because there was precious little of the latter; the two were quickly expelled from Guatemala. But in the eyes of many of their former Maryknoll colleagues, the negative effect of their crossing that line was that they granted unfounded legitimacy to the charge that *all* of Maryknoll's work in Central America was a cover for left-wing politics and revolutionary agitation.

The complex story of the Melville incident and its ramifications is beyond the scope of my purposes here. But the Melvilles' presence in Catonsville and the symbolic meaning they sought to ascribe to their actions there are directly relevant to the broader dynamic I am trying to describe. Here is an excerpt from a letter that Marjorie Melville sent to Tom at the time: "We've got to do something so that the U.S. people can understand what we're doing to the Guatemalan peasants. If we can convince young Americans not to seek their manhood in the Green Berets, or even better, persuade the American people not to finance counterinsurgency efforts in Latin America, we can save countless innocent people."[47]

The Melvilles' shift from pastoral concern into revolutionary violence was decidedly not typical of Maryknoll. But their overwhelming desire to educate their fellow citizens back in the United States about what they had seen, learned, and experienced in Central America certainly was. Indeed their search for ways to make the connection for US Catholics between suffering in Central America and US foreign policy became in time a hallmark of the Maryknoll approach to mission. For Tom and Marjorie Melville, that search led them to the symbolically rich antiwar activism of the Berrigan brothers, and to the hope that they could use that activism to draw attention to American policy in Central America. As Tom

Melville put it: They decided that they "would burn the draft files if it were indicated that our action was related to Guatemala and Latin America."[48]

Janice McLaughlin was another Maryknoll missioner who decided, in an entirely different context, that a large element of her mission was to prod her fellow US citizens to recognize the injustice that she was experiencing by living and working among the people. For McLaughlin those people were the black populations of southern Africa, and the particular injustice she sought to redress was the racial policies of Ian Smith's regime in Rhodesia (later Zimbabwe) and the tacit support that those policies received in the United States and elsewhere. Working as a press spokesperson for the Justice and Peace Commission in Rhodesia in the late 1970s, she was jailed, threatened with execution, and finally expelled from the country. No longer able to pursue political change directly through her work in Africa, McLaughlin, "good publicist that she was," in Penny Lernoux's words, "took the spotlight with her to Europe and the United States, denouncing the Smith regime without cessation . . . and raising money for the Rhodesian refugees exiled in Mozambique."[49] This particular Maryknoll missioner, exiled from her people in southern Africa, decided to devote herself to the tasks of reverse mission in her native United States. Like the Melvilles, though in a profoundly different way, Janice McLaughlin saw it as her direct responsibility as a missioner and a Christian to tell people back home what she knew—to implore people back home to insist on changes in the foreign policies that she saw as so very damaging to the people she had left her Pittsburgh home to serve.

The Ear of the Speaker

All of these activities were efforts to be what Oscar Romero said he wanted to be in El Salvador: "the voice of the voiceless." Peggy Healy, one of the most active Maryknoll sisters in Central America in the late 1970s and late 1980s, explicitly echoed Romero's words when describing what she and the other sisters were doing and why they were doing it: "We could allow the voice of the people we were working with to be heard," she said over two decades later. "[We could] be a voice for people who didn't have a voice."⁵⁰ In a way that was so clearly typical of the modern Maryknoll notion of mission, and so congruent with the Maryknollers' understanding of their responsibility to the people in Central America, Healy and the other sisters set out to evangelize their fellow citizens in the United States—to teach people in Hartford and Detroit and San Francisco what was actually happening in Guatemala, El Salvador, and Nicaragua.

The sisters did not start out with a conscious commitment to reverse mission. In the case of Peggy Healy, for example, the whole dynamic started in terms of practical, day-to-day efforts to protect her neighbors in Nicaragua from the repressive practices of Somoza's national guard. Her neighborhood had attracted the attention of the *guardia* (as it was called) following the fight over access to water mentioned earlier, and Healy found herself defending her neighbors—her people—when the *guardia* came to look for them. Fairly soon, however, she and a few of her colleagues took the crucial step of looking north for help, as they began to relay the testimony of their neighbors to a congressional committee in Washington that was at the time looking into the human rights record of the Nicaraguan regime. Working through WOLA, Healy and the others did all they could, in her words, "to represent the poor people, the dispossessed, those who didn't have a voice in their own society, much less in the United States."⁵¹

Peggy Healy's role in the United States and her commitment to reverse mission probably would not have gone beyond this modest but important role if not for a curious bit of timing and coincidence. Very resistant to leaving her post in Nicaragua, Healy was nevertheless ordered by her superiors back to Ossining in 1978 for a year of further theological study and personal reflection. When she returned to the United States, however, she resolved to continue to do everything she could to make people more aware of what she saw as the tragic circumstances in Central America and, just as importantly, of the very negative role she believed US foreign policy was playing in the region. She testified before Congress herself; she spoke at forums arranged by groups like WOLA and Oxfam; and she visited churches—Catholic and otherwise—to tell Christians in the United States what was being done to their fellow Christians in Nicaragua.

Then in 1979, with the Sandinista revolution cresting, and unable to return as a missioner to Nicaragua, Healy began a two-year stint as the head of WOLA in Washington, DC. While receiving what she calls a "fabulous education" in Washington, Healy also had an unprecedented opportunity to be a voice for the voiceless and, not incidentally, to try to do what she really wanted to do at the time: "to change US policy." "There was nothing hidden about it," she said in our interview of her lobbying efforts to increase pressure on the US government to take note of Somoza's dismal human rights record and then, after the revolution had succeeded, to get the US government to "give the new government [in Nicaragua] a chance" by following through with millions of dollars of foreign aid that was already in the pipeline.[52]

Healy recalls now how anxious she was at the time to speak carefully and accurately about the lives being lived by the people in Nicaragua to whom she passionately hoped to return soon. But she also recalls how important she thought it was that she could speak also "about [her] experiences as a US citizen." "As US citizens," she said in our interview, "we felt we had a particular role to play in this because it was our country, and because we had access and the experience, and also we had a certain position of credibility."[53] As it turned out, no Maryknoll sister and very few activists of any kind have ever had the level of access Peggy Healy had at that time in Washington, DC. And that access, as she understood it then and since, was based almost entirely on the credibility she readily enjoyed as a Maryknoll missioner. Thomas P. (Tip) O'Neill (D-MA), Speaker of the House of Representatives from 1975 to 1986, happened to be the nephew of Sister Eunice, a Maryknoll sister by then in retirement in Ossining. Healy knew Eunice well, so when Healy returned from Nicaragua and began her work in Washington, the younger sister was told by her older colleague to "go and see my nephew, and tell him that I sent you to see him." Healy did indeed go and see Tip O'Neill, and the Maryknoll sister and the Speaker of the House embarked on a long relationship of mutual trust whereby Peggy Healy served as a back channel source of information and analysis on what was going on in Central America and on the impact of US policy on the people who lived in the region.

As Allen Hertzke put it in discussing Maryknoll influence on O'Neill, this was a "form of political access money cannot buy."[54] In her own words, Healy had "the ear of the Speaker," and she used her access to O'Neill to "keep him abreast of what was going on" in Nicaragua and El Salvador.[55] This was not a single formal meeting between a representative and a constituent. This was an ongoing relationship and interaction that lasted for a number of years and continued even after Healy returned to Central America in 1981 to serve as the regional director for all of Maryknoll's activities there. "I kept in very close contact with the Speaker," she said in our interview, "sending him things, and whenever I went back to the states I would visit him and keep him abreast of what was going on."[56] In short order, of course, the main policy controversy in Central America morphed from the question of whether to support the new regime in Nicaragua to the much more urgent question of whether to fund and support the contras, the counterrevolutionary movement that was waging war against the Sandinistas with the active support of President Reagan.

Speaker O'Neill was an insistent and outspoken opponent of US support for the contras, and he was not at all hesitant in saying where the motivation for that opposition came from. "I have a connection with the Maryknoll order," he said at the time. "I have great respect for that order. When the nuns and priests come through I ask them about their feelings, what they see, who the enemy is, and I am sure I get the truth. I haven't found any of these missionaries who aren't absolutely opposed to this policy [of funding the contras]."[57] Putting an even finer point on the matter, the Speaker also said publicly: "Am I wrong listening to women who live in Nicaragua and follow the Sermon on the Mount? Or am I supposed to sit here and believe generals?"[58] James Wright (D-TX), then majority leader of the House and a close associate of O'Neill's, remembers

Healy's insistence in her meetings and communications with them that the contras were absolutely wicked, and Wright believed that Healy's clarity and credibility were important factors in solidifying the Speaker's opposition to Reagan's policy.[59]

As with the Jesuits' role in cutting funding for the Salvadoran military a few years later, Peggy Healy's role in generating opposition to the contras was one of providing texture and justification for a position that O'Neill and other political opponents of Ronald Reagan might well have arrived at through other means. But the testimony of US missionaries, nuns who were presumed by many (though not all) Americans to be above petty political motivation, was a powerful tool for the Speaker of the House. The possibly apocryphal story is often told of an exchange between Reagan and O'Neill when the two leaders were having a personal discussion about the contras, Reagan's "moral equal to our Founding Fathers."[60] Expressing frustration at O'Neill's resistance to his arguments, President Reagan offered with exasperation that he was basing his own convictions on accurate information given to him by the CIA. "Well," the Speaker supposedly deadpanned, "my information is much more accurate than that. I get mine from nuns."

The kind of information that O'Neill was receiving from Peggy Healy, and the passion with which that information was conveyed, were both captured in a letter, sent from Healy to O'Neill in 1984, that the Speaker passed on to the *New York Times*: "The war that is happening in Central America right now," she wrote from her post in the region, "and which threatens to escalate and bring even more disaster, challenges us—all of us who believe in Jesus—to follow the words of Paul in Ephesians: 'So stand your ground, with truth buckled around your waist and integrity as a breastplate, wearing for shoes on your feet the eagerness to spread the gospel of peace and always carrying the shield of faith so that you can use it to put out the burning arrows of the evil one.'"[61] Not exactly the usual fare in the world of Washington lobbying. But by all accounts, this was an effective method of motivating a politician like O'Neill, who adored his Aunt Eunice and who had "great respect for [the Maryknoll] order."[62]

The Moral Responsibility of Our Country

Needless to say, Peggy Healy's opportunity to advance the cause of the people of Central America along the corridors of power in Washington, DC, was a unique phenomenon. Even she spent most of her time in this regard not conferring with high government leaders, but instead working through WOLA to seek changes in US policy or speaking to community and church groups across the country to raise awareness about what was happening in "our own backyard." Many other Maryknoll sisters did the same when they made their way north to take on administrative tasks in Ossining or to reconnect with their families and the larger Maryknoll community during their periodically mandated visits home. The sisters told their stories, extolled the goodness of the people, and described, in classic missionary style and in unflinching terms, what Christian faith and a Christian conscience required of their listeners.

But no one told a more dramatic story, or cut a less likely public figure, than Nancy Donovan. The "sister with spunk," according to the *Catholic New York* newspaper—the "Maryknoll nun kidnapped in Nicaragua [while] trying to help others"—never minced her words after her kidnapping gave her a prominent platform from which to speak.[63] The contras who had detained her were "terrorists"; US funding of them was "immoral"; President Reagan would have to "answer to God" for "the diabolical acts" he was supporting; and "the hope [that] we live with" is that "when the American people stand up and say 'enough,' it will be stopped."[64]

Nancy Donovan was a reluctant celebrity. She said, "When I made that decision of getting off that pickup truck and heading off into Contra-controlled territory, I thought a lot of things could happen to me—I could be killed or I could be kidnapped, but I did not think that what would happen would be international fame."[65] But from the very first minute, she used the notoriety that came her way in 1985 to focus the public's attention on the plight of the people in Nicaragua, and to do so explicitly as an American citizen. In her first press conference, held shortly after she was released in January 1985, she said, "As a Christian and as an American citizen I feel great pain for the fact that my government has been responsible for the arming and training of these forces which have caused the deaths of so many."[66] And as she traveled that year speaking at dozens of forums and workshops at churches and community centers all over the United States, she always focused on the same themes. The first and most prominent was the requirement that US citizens be held accountable not only for what was being done by their government in countries far away, but also for the state of democracy in their own country. "I'm talking about the moral responsibility of our country," Donovan said at Wayne State University in Michigan. "If the majority of the people oppose the politicians and are vocal about it and still the administration doesn't change then I think that this is something we have to look at very carefully. We're saying that the democratic process in this administration doesn't work."[67]

Another prominent theme was just how difficult life was in northern Nicaragua, and just how much more difficult the contra war was making it. "Our biggest job," she said in Louisville, Kentucky, "is burying the dead, and consoling the grieving. . . . I work with the poor, live with them, bury them, love them. I see their struggles. I support them in their search for a new, better way of life."[68] And in her hometown of Waterbury, Connecticut, she was even more blunt: The intent of the contras, she said, was "to terrorize, to kidnap, to torture, to kill. It is quite horrible living there."[69] Making direct reference to President Reagan's presentation of the contras as "freedom fighters," Donovan asked, "What kind of freedom is it they are seeking by raping and killing women, torturing men, kidnapping boys and ruining villages? These are being done daily," she reminded her listeners at Sacred Heart High School, "by forces financed by the U.S. government."[70] "We are killing people all through Latin America," she said later in New Mexico, "and the U.S. public should be indignant about it."[71]

Finally, Nancy Donovan took it upon herself, as part of her mission in the United States, to provide a counterbalance to what she saw as the unfair demonization of the Sandinista government by the Reagan administration and the US press. While always couching her comments in calibrated terms that recognized the "imperfections" of the revolutionary government, the Maryknoll missioner was anxious to tell her listeners about the gains that had been made in areas such as literacy and community development since the Somoza dictatorship had been overthrown. The American public is "being lied to," she said, and therefore they were not aware that the Sandinistas were "really, sincerely on the side of the poor."[72] Acknowledging that US politicians "don't want to be called 'soft on Communism'—that's about the worst you could be called by anyone these days," she argued that "all sorts of immoral acts are being done for fear of being soft on communism."[73] Rejecting outright the argument that the Nicaraguan revolution was communist in form or inspiration, Donovan retreated to a predictable emphasis on the views and aspirations of the ordinary Nicaraguan people. "You ask these people," she said one night in Connecticut, "'Are you a Communist?' And they look at you like, 'what's that?'"[74]

It was this last effort—this attempt to put a human face on the Sandinistas, and the attempt to argue that the new Nicaraguan government was better than the old one and worthy of US support—that proved at the time to be most controversial. Sisters like Nancy Donovan and Peggy Healy were called naive and worse for supporting a government with which the United States was all but at war. It is true, as it was charged at the time, that the sisters did more than oppose the US effort to destabilize the Sandinista government; they affirmatively supported that government. I probably should not have been surprised to find in Nancy Donovan's personal papers a certificate naming her as an "honorary member of the Sandinista Front," saved among all of the press clippings of her kidnapping and her subsequent missionary tour of the United States. This, after all, was the woman who had praised the levels of freedom in the new Nicaragua, declaring that "just as in America, all religious sects are free to function in Nicaragua."[75] She had also scoffed at the idea of the Sandinistas as terrorists, saying that if that use of the loaded term was legitimate, then "I need a new dictionary."[76] And perhaps most tellingly she also said that the Sandinista revolution had left her "excited about the possibility of constructively building a new society." But, she said, because of US opposition and the contra war, she was instead spending a lot of her time "consoling those who have lost people dear to them."[77]

This was just the kind of rhetoric that led people like William Buckley at the *National Review* to characterize the Maryknoll sisters as being in the thrall of "Christian Marxism,"[78] and author Michael Novak to say that the entire Maryknoll order was "promoting Christian Marxism—uncritically, naively, grandly, extensively."[79] And it was the sort of criticism of the very bases of US foreign policy that led men like William Casey, the director of the Central Intelligence Agency under President Reagan, to be "driven crazy" by the nuns, in the words of Peggy Healy. But to a woman like Nancy Donovan, it was all a fundamental part of what she saw as her responsibility as a Christian, as a missioner, and as a US citizen.

When the Jesuit priests were killed at the UCA in San Salvador, their fellow members in the Society of Jesus within the United States did what they knew how to do and what they had the resources to do. They organized themselves, *universidadamente*, and approached their US government to try to get it to deal more aggressively with a Salvadoran government that had killed "six of ours." In some ways the Maryknoll sisters did similar things, though with a different focus and with different resources. To be sure, when Maura Clarke and Ita Ford were killed outside San Salvador in 1980, the order responded with its own sense of personal grief and its own insistence that the US government work with the Congregation to pressure the Salvadorans to investigate. But on the whole, the Maryknoll sisters responded to the horrors they experienced in Central America with their own distinctive approach, their own distinctively mission-based approach. Their clear commitment to accompanying the poor in their suffering, coupled with their very real appreciation of their responsibilities as US citizens, led them to go out once again, two by two: not in rural China this time, but rather in suburban America to try to change hearts and convert people to a deeper, more active form of Christianity.

Peggy Healy, as she often did in the 1970s and 1980s, put it most directly and most eloquently in an interview with me more than twenty years after the fact. Echoing once again Oscar Romero's claim to be "the voice of the voiceless," and speaking of the varied and energetic efforts at reverse mission in the 1980s taken up by her and the other Maryknollers in Central America, she said, "Your job

was not to change US foreign policy because it was entirely unenlightened, although it was entirely unenlightened. Your job was to
try to be a voice for people who were suffering because of it. It had
to be changed because of the day-to-day results of it. Not once in a
while, not in some vague way, but every single day it affected their
survival. It needed to be changed, and in the end that was the reason
why we did it."[80]

Or as Nancy Donovan told me over lunch one day in Ossining:
Her government was killing *her* people, and the only question was,
What was she going to do about it? The answer, at its base, was that
she was going to be what she had been since she was a teenager: She
was going to be a missionary. She was going to come "home" from
Nicaragua and evangelize the United States and in a new way try to
"go to the ends of the earth to spread the Good News of the reign of
God."[81] She was going to tell her fellow citizens in the United States
what they were doing to her people in Nicaragua, and she was going
to ask those citizens to convert their hearts. I doubt that anyone trying to change American foreign policy could put their policy pro-
posals in more personal terms than that. And I also doubt that any
ethnic lobbyist or rooted cosmopolitan could express a deeper level
of connectedness with non-Americans than the transnational solidarity expressed by this group of women as they carried out their
reverse mission on behalf of their people.

CHAPTER 4

Hospitality

A Covenant between
Mexico and Vermont

Known as the "City of Eternal Spring" because of its spectacular year-round weather, Cuernavaca, Mexico, is also notable for its abundant natural beauty—and for its equally abundant, but not always equally visible, local poverty. Amid the hundreds of restaurants serving prosperous Mexicans and visiting tourists, Cuernavaca also features countless children hawking gum, row after row of women selling fruit and fabric, and whole stretches of urban landscape where the sturdiest structure is made of scrap metal walls and a tarpaper roof. Through its own diversity, Cuernavaca serves as a kind of living symbol of Mexico's own complex identity as a developing Latin American country that shares a lengthy international border with the richest country in the world. Cuernavaca's lovely lanes and orderly *zocalo*, or town square, illustrate the economic advantages that accrue to Mexico from being so close to the United States. But Cuernavaca's homeless children and hopeless peasants also illustrate how unevenly those economic advantages are distributed in Mexico, and how multidimensional Mexico's relationship is with its colossal neighbor to the north.

A mile or so up one of those lovely lanes from that tidy *zocalo* sits the Guadalupe Center, a place that serves as both the home of a small group of Benedictine sisters who have devoted their lives to serving Mexico's poor and as the site of a transnational religious project that has the ambitious goal of introducing visitors, "especially from the United States and Canada," to the reality of life and poverty as they are actually lived in Latin America. This small group of women in Cuernavaca is part of a much larger community of Benedictine sisters called Las Misioneras Guadalupanas de Cristo Rey, centered in Mexico City. But the sisters at the Guadalupe Center in Cuernavaca are also on the front lines of a deep and long-lasting transnational relationship between the Guadalupanas of Mexico and a group of Benedictine monks who live at the Weston Priory in rural Vermont. Opened in 1984 as a joint venture between the sisters of Mexico and the brothers of Vermont, the Guadalupe Center and its programs are only the most tangible and visible manifestations of a communal relationship that the sisters and brothers all refer to as their covenant, or Arco Iris de Alianza.[1]

Committed to "walking with each other" into an uncertain future and "accompanying" each other on a shared pathway of Benedictine spirituality and social justice, these two Benedictine communities are constantly looking for ways in which they can draw themselves closer to each other, use their relationship to inform and instruct others about the Benedictine principle of hospitality, and make a meaningful contribution to transforming relationships across the United States–Mexico border that they see as deeply damaging to the Mexican people.[2] At one level the Alianza is a simple compact between two groups of people seeking support and fellowship as they live their communal lives according to the Rule of Saint Benedict. At the same time, the Alianza is also a politically charged cross-border religious affiliation that seeks to apply the principles of that Rule to modern economics, modern politics, and contemporary US foreign policy. These Benedictine brothers and sisters are quite modest in lifestyle and affect. They are anything but modest, however, in their hopes for social, economic, and political change in the United States and also especially in Latin America.

The Rule

As we have seen in each of the case studies included in this book, transnational religious communities have a glue that holds them together, a shared foundation that ties large groups of men and women to each other across time and geographic space. For the

Jesuits, it is their shared formation through the Spiritual Exercises of Saint Ignatius of Loyola; for the Maryknollers, it is their shared commitment to a life of mission in solidarity with the life and suffering of the people. All of these ties, as we have seen, are powerful and meaningful. But no such glue or foundation has been more integrative or longer-lasting than that which binds Benedictines all over the world through their shared devotion and submission to the Rule of Saint Benedict.

The Rule—as it is universally known—was written in the sixth century by Saint Benedict of Nursia, the founder of Monte Cassino Monastery in Italy, and one of the leading monastic teachers and leaders in the Western Christian tradition. Still vibrantly alive after 1,400 years of reform and reformulation, the Rule continues to structure the communal lives of the priests, lay brothers, and nuns who live in the thousands of Benedictine monasteries throughout the world. These monasteries vary substantially by cultural region and by degree of what might be called severity or observance. But all Benedictines, wherever they may be and however they may be living, subscribe to Saint Benedict's opening dictum that prayer is "the first step of anything worthwhile."[3]

Benedictines are not "contemplatives in action," the phrase used to describe the Jesuits and sometimes even the Maryknollers. Instead, Benedictines are simply contemplatives, or more specifically cenobites, religious men and women who, according to Benedict, are "based in a monastery and fulfill their service to the Lord under a rule and an abbot or abbess."[4] These days, Benedictine communities can be quite small (the brothers in Weston number only twelve) or rather large (membership in the Misioneras Guadalupanas numbers more than two hundred). Some communities (like the Mexican sisters) are quite active in pastoral work, operating schools and orphanages and social service agencies with which any Jesuit priest or Maryknoll missioner would be entirely familiar. Others (such as the Weston Priory) are far more traditional in approach, focusing their energies and defining their role in the Church as one of prayer, work, and the distinctly Benedictine principle of hospitality. But all are Benedictines, and all share a life defined and structured by the Rule.

The Rule, not surprisingly, is full of rules, many of which one would expect to find in the constitution of a religious community. "Don't get too involved in worldly affairs," the Rule orders, for example, "and count nothing more important than the love you should cherish for Christ." But many of the rules in the Rule focus on seemingly the most mundane of matters. "Don't drink to excess or overeat," it instructs, and "don't be lazy, nor give way to excessive sleep." "Don't be a murmurer," the Rule warns, because persistent grumbling is the bane of monastic community. Some very specific instructions have been consigned to the past, of course. Do all Benedictines, for example, still "sleep in their normal clothes, wearing a belt or cord around their waists?" I know from my own visits to Benedictine houses that the order to "fulfill that sacred number of seven" by pausing for communal prayers seven times each day is not always respected. And rare is the Benedictine community in the twenty-first century that "arises at the eighth hour of the night" during wintertime, given that in Benedict's time, the eighth hour of the night conformed to what we would call 2:40 a.m. today![5]

But the spirit of the Rule very much lives on, and that spirit is still manifested with significant specificity. The Benedictine communities in Vermont and Mexico do still keep the hours by gathering several times a day for communal prayer, if not always seven times. Both communities have a deep respect for the Rule's injunction that "silence should be sought at all times by monks and nuns," and both place manual labor and the *lectio divina* (a traditional practice of spiritual reading) at the center of their communal lives in response to the Rule's admonition that "idleness is the enemy of the soul." Finally—and, as we shall see, crucially for the circumstances I detail in this chapter—the bedrock commitment to hospitality and the reception of guests remains a foundational aspect of Benedictine spirituality among the monks in Weston and the sisters in Cuernavaca and Mexico City. Saint Benedict decreed that "any guest who happens to arrive at the monastery should be received just as we would receive Christ himself," and that is exactly what the brothers and sisters work to provide for people who come to stay with them in Vermont and Mexico.[6]

Benedictines throughout the world are also consistently characterized by a commitment to what they call "stability," an individual
decision to live one's life in *this* place, with *these* brothers or sisters,
as part of *this* specific local community. In this way the vocation of
a Benedictine man or woman differs at its very core from the vocations associated with the other communities we have examined thus
far. Unlike Jesuits and their ideal of mobility, for example, or Maryknollers and their insistence on traveling to find the people who
need their mission the most, Benedictines are profoundly rooted
in a specific place: wedded to a specific community, and committed
to living an entire life of work, prayer, and hospitality in (usually) a
single monastery.

This principle of stability has wide-ranging ramifications for the
nature of Benedictine organization and for the way that transnational connections between and among Benedictines are articulated
and structured. Benedictine communication and solidarity is often
expressed community to community, or house to house. Brothers
and sisters do not lose their personal identities, of course, and many
Benedictines work, speak, and travel as individuals, separate and
apart from the local communities or monasteries to which they belong. But in ways that would be foreign to Jesuits, for example, Benedictines interact with each other in a community-to-community
sense as well. As we will see with the Arco Iris de Alianza between
Vermont and Mexico, this transnational relationship is not between
Brother X and Sister Y, or even between this group of brothers and
that group of sisters. It is instead a solemn and formal covenant between two communities, founded and nourished by a common life
under the Rule of Saint Benedict and by a common understanding of the meaning and ramifications of contemporary Benedictine
spirituality. The covenant between Vermont and Mexico is formally
renewed every few years by the brothers and sisters who compose
the community at that time (and to be sure, many members of both
communities have been present throughout the relationship). But
the Alianza itself is neither dependent on nor limited to the men
and women who live in Vermont or Mexico at a given moment.
Instead, it is an ongoing communal commitment, meant to emphasize the collective nature of each side of the relationship and to

embody a specifically Benedictine way of understanding covenant and friendship.

Stability also deeply affects the way Benedictines organize themselves as an international order. The commitments to local community and stability are so foundational that Benedictines do not actually constitute an "order" as that term is generally understood in the Catholic lexicon. Instead, transnational Benedictinism is better defined as a loosely affiliated confederation made up of relatively autonomous local houses that are, for the most part, grouped into national or supranational congregations. For the male side of the Benedictine experience, there are currently twenty-one of these congregations, all coordinated, but not exactly governed, by an elected abbot primate who resides in Rome. Each monastery is ruled by an individual abbot; each congregation is overseen by a president; and the abbot primate plays a coordinating role by facilitating communication and cooperation among and between Benedictines living all over the globe. It is important to emphasize that this structure is much less hierarchical than, for example, the transnational ordering of the Jesuits reviewed in chapter 2. The abbot primate is not another "general," governing a cohesive society through assistants and provincials who are answerable to him in any sort of formal ecclesiastical sense. The abbot primate is more like a living symbol of Benedictine solidarity, a spiritual guide who spends much of his time traveling around the globe visiting individual houses, monasteries, and congregations so that he can evaluate the health and status of the Benedictine community in a given place at a given time.

Female Benedictines are even less closely governed from a center of authority than their male counterparts are. Usually "associated" with the male congregations but not formally members of them, Benedictine women exist, frankly, in a kind of uncertain space within the broader community structures. They are Benedictines, to be sure; their commitment to the Rule is enough to establish that. But these female houses are often quite autonomous, sometimes substantially cut off from other Benedictines due to the fact that they are organized into individual congregations that are even less tied to the Benedictine Confederation and the abbot primate than male communities are. Rembert Weakland, who served as abbot

primate from 1967 to 1977 (when he became archbishop of Milwaukee), told me in an interview that one of his greatest challenges as
abbot primate was keeping in close touch with Benedictine women,
making sure not only that they were being well treated in their local environments but also that they were sufficiently integrated into
Benedictine structures and support systems.[7]

Weakland also told me that he had been particularly concerned,
in this regard, about the relative isolation of the Guadalupanas in
Mexico, and he had sought ways as abbot primate to serve their
long-term interests by integrating them more fully into the larger
Benedictine world. In fact, he had had similar concerns about the
brothers of the Weston Priory in Vermont. In their case Weakland
was not necessarily concerned that the community in Weston was
inappropriately isolated from transnational Benedictine structures
per se. Rather, he felt that the brothers' wholly admirable devotion
to a more traditional monastic regimen and understanding of stability threatened to render their community life in Vermont overly
insular and therefore potentially stale. Grasping the opportunity to
address both concerns at the same time, Weakland set the Alianza in
motion in 1973 when he suggested that the brothers from Vermont
pay a visit to the sisters in Mexico. He told the monks of the Weston
Priory that they would discover a shared spirit with the women in
Mexico, and that both communities would benefit from interacting
with each other. Typical of internal Benedictine relations, the abbot primate left entirely up to the brothers and the sisters how to
shape or articulate that interaction. And to be sure, neither Weakland nor the members of the two communities had any idea what a
life-shaping experience his suggested meeting would turn out to be
for all concerned.

The Brothers

The Weston Priory, a monastic community of a dozen men in rural
Vermont, is an anomaly, relatively speaking, in terms of its structural
relationship to the rest of the Benedictine Confederation. Weston is
one of only fourteen monasteries throughout the world that are not
members of a broader and larger congregation. Known formally as

a *monasterium monachrurum extra congregational,* this small monastery is an "individual conventual priory" under the direct jurisdiction of the abbot primate in Rome.[8] In practice, given its small size and geographic isolation, this structural peculiarity makes the Weston Priory remarkably, and almost entirely, autonomous. This circumstance is derived from the priory's rather unusual history. Never intended by its founder to evolve into an independent monastic community, the Weston Priory was for the first fifteen years or so of its existence associated with a place called Dormition Abbey in Jerusalem, Israel.[9] Weston was founded in 1953 by the abbot of Dormition, a German monk by the name of Leo Rudloff, and the Weston Priory was at the beginning conceived of as a kind of feeder monastery, an American outpost where potential monks could be identified and trained for the purpose of integrating them into the much larger Benedictine community under Abbot Leo's leadership in the Holy Land.[10]

Abbot Leo, a man of grand vision—and for a time equally grand ambition—desired to spark at Weston no less than a wholesale reformation—or better stated as "reassertion," from his point of view—of the Benedictine monastic tradition. Disappointed with the degree to which Saint Benedict's Rule had been bent and stretched to accommodate pastoral work and external engagement on the part of Benedictine monks, Leo wanted to return to a more traditional approach to *ora et labora,* prayer and work, as the heart of monastic life. Weston was to be the experimental laboratory of this effort at restoration, a place of "monastic presence rooted in hospitality, prayer," and "faithfulness to the Rule of Benedict."[11] And from Weston new monks, devoted to this more traditional form of Benedictine monasticism, could be sent out to the broader Benedictine community. Central to this vision of reform was Abbot Leo's insistence on erasing the distinction that had grown over time between "choir monks" and "lay brothers." In most Benedictine communities, choir monks, all of whom were ordained priests, would carry out the pastoral functions and many of the monastic functions of the community, while lay brothers, unordained lay men, would support those activities through the manual labor that such a community required. Abbot Leo felt very strongly that this distinction violated Benedictine principles in both directions—it exempted priests from much of the labor that was meant to be at the heart of the monastery's life, and it alienated the lay men from the brotherhood and community that all Benedictines were intended to share. At his monastery—or at least at the priory built to support it—members of the community, ordained and lay, would share equally in all of the *labora* and all of the *ora*, and the members of the community would always address each other equally and simply as "brother."[12]

Dormition Abbey itself was a fascinating place in the 1950s and 1960s, and it was the instrument of Leo Rudloff's other grand design: a deeper engagement between Christianity and Judaism, as well as the use of monastic space in the Holy Land as the embodiment of Benedictine respect for the Jewish religion and of post-Holocaust reconciliation with the Jewish people. The hope of populating this abbey with monks trained in Vermont was an inspired and noble one, but it ultimately failed, or in Abbot Leo's own words, "faded out completely."[13] No monk who was formed in Vermont ever settled at Dormition Abbey; and despite enormous effort expended by Abbot Leo over many years, the organic relationship between the two monasteries never took hold outside of his fervent desires. What very much did take hold in Weston, however, was Leo's reformation and restoration of monastic structure through the elimination of what he viewed as the pernicious distinction between choir monks and lay brothers. This egalitarian approach was indeed revolutionary for its time, and an ethos of communal equality was firmly established at Weston. In fact, a conscious assertion of monastic equalitarianism served as a central element of the priory's own communal identity once it became clear that Weston could only survive as a monastic community on the basis of its own unique character, and not in association with Dormition Abbey of Jerusalem. Abbot Leo was deeply disappointed in the failure of his cherished association between Weston and Jerusalem to take root, and in truth he himself did not always find it easy to leave the distinctions of rank and hierarchy behind in his personal day-to-day dealings with his fellow monks.[14] But it is nevertheless a central element of the Weston Priory's history and development that Leo Rudloff resigned as abbot of

Dormition in 1968 and lived out the rest of his years until he died in 1982 on that quiet hillside in Vermont, living, working, and praying as Brother Leo.[15]

The other aspect of Leo's vision that survived in Weston, not without some controversy, was his desire to rededicate monastic life to the prayer and work of the monastery rather than to pastoral work outside of it. These days, in the United States and throughout the world, many Benedictine monastics can be found running and staffing colleges like Jesuits do, and furthering social goals in hospitals, orphanages, and elsewhere like Maryknollers do. These activities can themselves be manifestations of the Benedictine value of hospitality, but these activities also necessarily disrupt the rhythms of monastic observance and draw those who engage in them away from the pervasive silence and contemplation of the monastic life. The Weston Priory was founded explicitly for the purpose of reaffirming those traditional rhythms and silences, and the brothers have never adopted pastoral duties as they are generally defined. There is no Weston Priory School or Weston University, no affiliated hospital, and no regular work outside the priory carried out by any of its members. That is not to say that the brothers force upon themselves an isolation as pervasive as their silence, but it does mean that they are powerfully attuned to the ways in which they and their monastic values are connected to the world outside their gates.

One way that these connections are maintained is through the now rather famous music produced and recorded by the brothers. All Benedictine communities are expected to be as self-sufficient as possible in financial terms. Those with external apostolates can sometimes reap the profits of their work outside the walls of the monastery, in universities, hospitals, and so on. But for more enclosed communities like Weston, funds must often be procured through the manufacture and sale of products that the monks or nuns make themselves within the community. Some readers might be aware of relatively well-known merchandise like Monks Bread, Benedictine Wine, Trappist Preserves—or the music of the Monks of Weston Priory. After relatively unsuccessful forays in dairy farming ("those cows milked us," they told me) and other forms of living off the land, the brothers found over time that there was a substantial commercial market for the distinctive music that they composed and sang at their communal prayer services. Closer to modern folk music than traditional monastic chant, their music has brought the brothers considerable fame (and I imagine at least some measure of fortune). But in earlier days the music also posed a number of troubling challenges to the community. How public should the brothers be in terms of their music? How open should the monastery be to those who came to listen to them sing? How should the brothers react to the social and political activists who sought out Weston's songs as the spiritual background music for their meetings and protests?[16]

It was in this context that Rembert Weakland, the Benedictines' abbot primate, decided to nudge the Weston brothers in a different direction by encouraging them to turn just a bit from their insular debates and endeavors to more actively engage Benedictine communities in other social and cultural circumstances. Most monasteries are forced outside themselves a bit by their membership in a broader congregation. But fully autonomous communities like the Weston Priory—and for that matter the Misioneras Guadalupanas de Cristo Rey—need to seek out engagement with the broader confederation a bit more actively. This, really, was what Weakland had in mind for the brothers in Vermont and the sisters in Mexico. But Weakland also had in mind that Benedictines in the "new world" of the Americas should not focus as much of their attention as was customary on the Benedictines in the "old world" of Europe. Perhaps as a function of his status as the only abbot primate to come from the United States, Weakland wished to foster and encourage interaction between the United States and Latin America in the hope of sparking dialogue over monastic renewal outside the European context and history.

The monks of the Weston Priory, it should be said, were very much open to this message at the time it was delivered. They were in the process in the early 1970s of establishing their own connections with Latin America, particularly through their support of a gentleman from Vermont (and his Chilean wife) who were performing lay ministry, portentously as it turned out, in the City of Eternal Spring in Mexico.[17] In fact, the monks were planning to travel to Cuernavaca to learn more about this ministry firsthand and to explore other ways in which they could interact with the exciting theological and pastoral work that was then being done within the Catholic Church in Latin America.[18] In so many ways the stage was set for the meeting that Weakland suggested: a meeting between two groups of thoroughly independent Benedictines who would recognize right away that their two communities shared what the brothers refer to as a "common spirit" and the sisters define as *el propio carisma*.[19]

Las Hermanas

The Misioneras Guadalupanas de Cristo Rey were indeed well disposed to respond positively to Weakland's suggestion that they make the acquaintance of the Benedictine monks from Weston.[20] The community of Guadalupanas, comprising more than two hundred women, is quite a bit larger than the monastery in Weston; and unlike the single monastic home occupied by the brothers in Vermont, the Mexican sisters are rather broadly dispersed, residing in their *casa central* in Mexico City as well as in their many missions around Mexico and the neighboring countries of Central America. In addition, the sisters, because of the work implied by the title *misioneras*, are much more outward-looking than the brothers are, devoting much greater time and energy than the brothers do to duties and commitments outside of their monastic walls.

Despite these substantial differences in organization and outlook, however, the two communities also have a great deal in common. Of greatest importance to the brothers and sisters is what they all take to be their shared spirit, their common devotion to the accessible spirituality and equalitarian communal life that led Weakland to link the two communities in his mind in the first place. But perhaps of equal importance is the fact that the two communities also share a profound level of institutional autonomy—and a certain distance from the formal structures of the Benedictine Confederation that led each of them to develop their own unique communal ethos, but that also imposed on each of them what Weakland took to be an unfortunate level of isolation from the broader Benedictine world. These shared commitments and this common experience of institutional autonomy combined to create an immediate sense of recognition and affinity when the two communities met in 1976.

The best way to convey the complex history of the Misioneras Guadalupanas de Cristo Rey is to take each word of the name in turn, recognize how each is laden with meaning, and see how each word is connected to the others to form a communal title that conveys, with remarkable clarity, the ways in which this community is embedded in a deep intersection of its Mexican national heritage with its Benedictine congregational home. The two women recognized by the sisters as their foundress and cofoundress embodied this intersection both in their personal relationship to one another and in the roles that each played in the history of the community. The foundress, Mother Josefina María Valencia, represents the sisters' definitional status as Guadalupanas, which is to say devotees of Our Lady of Guadalupe and all that *la Virgen* represents in terms of Mexican history, culture, and spirituality. Cofoundress Mother María Placida Barrios de los Ríos, on the other hand, represents the decision by the sisters to pursue that quintessentially Mexican devotion and to structure their communal life and prayer according to the same Rule of Saint Benedict that directs the schedule and activities of the Weston Priory in rural Vermont. This combination of influences and commitments places a form of religious transnationalism right at the heart of the sisters' communal life. In one sense, the Guadalupanas' founding as a self-consciously *Mexican* religious community makes them as rooted a group of religious actors as one is likely to find anywhere. But in an equally important sense, their compliance with the Rule and their ready openness to a deep relationship with Benedictines from the north render them remarkably cosmopolitan in both outlook and experience.[21]

The first word of their name, *misioneras*, indicates that this group of Benedictine women is a community of just that: missionaries. Much like the Maryknoll sisters discussed in chapter 3, and quite unlike their Benedictine brothers in Vermont, the Guadalupanas are devoted to the active apostolate of bringing the teachings of Jesus Christ to those who would otherwise not have access to them. As we saw earlier, this commitment is defined in our modern era more in terms of accompanying the people of God, and less in

terms of converting souls to the Catholic Church. In fact, the Guadalupanas had precisely this sort of modern mission in mind from
the very start of their communal life together. José del Pilar Cas-
tellón Velasco, the Mexican priest whom the sisters call their "initiator," explicitly referred to the social teachings of Leo XIII's *Rerum
novarum* when he asked Josefina María Valencia in 1926 to found a
community of *misioneras* who would work with him in building the
"social kingdom" of God among the poor people of Mexico. This
explicit focus on Mexico at the community's founding, by the way,
was consciously intended by both initiator and foundress. Whereas
Maryknollers have always gone out from Ossining, New York, "to
the end of the earth to spread the Good News of the Reign of God,"
the Guadalupanas are rooted in a context and a mission that were
distinctively Mexican in both scope and devotion right from the
very beginning.[22]

   To be sure, the Mexican sisters have opened missions in Nicaragua, Guatemala, and even in the United States of America over the
years of their existence. But when the Guadalupanas were initiated
in 1926 and then were formally founded in 1930, the idea was to
create a community of women who would go out from the Basilica
of Our Lady of Guadalupe (their *casa central* is still only blocks from
the iconic church in Mexico City) to defend the Catholic identity of
the Mexican population and to preserve that population's specific
devotion to Our Lady of Guadalupe. *La Virgen*, as she is colloquially
and universally known throughout Mexico, revealed herself in an
apparition in 1531 to Juan Diego, a simple peasant whose life and
faithfulness also play a central role in Mexican Catholic tradition
(or mythology, I suppose, depending on your point of view). That
the Mother of Christ appeared, not to a Spanish prince or even to
an exalted Catholic bishop, but rather to an indigenous Mexican
peasant has come to serve as the heart of a national narrative holding that the Blessed Virgin associates herself with the poor people of
Mexico and with the historical aspirations of the Mexican people.
The word *guadalupanas* was meant to powerfully identify the sisters
with this national narrative and with its implications for the poor
people of the country. The sisters live (many of them literally) in
the shadow of Juan Diego's sacred cloak in the Basilica of Our Lady

of Guadalupe, and they remain devoted to the idea of articulating their mission and building the social kingdom of God through the imagery (and, they would argue, the intercession) of Mexico's clearest and most widely accepted national symbol.[23]

The sisters' specifically Mexican identity, however, goes even beyond this foundational connection to Our Lady of Guadalupe. The next phrase in their name, *Cristo Rey*, also has deep roots in Mexican history and also was a central motivational force behind their founding and development almost a century ago. The years 1926–30, after all, constitute a specific period in Mexican history when the so-called Ley Calles (named after President Plutarco Elías Calles) imposed radical restrictions on the public life of the Catholic Church in Mexico. The Church was stripped of all of its land holdings and was barred from any participation whatsoever in the educational institutions of the country. Moreover, monasteries were closed, foreign priests were expelled from the country, and Mexican priests were barred from any participation in public life, even from wearing clerical garb away from church grounds. It was in this specific context that Mother Josefina Valencia committed to founding a community of religious women who would oppose through their very existence the antireligious policies of the Mexican government, but who would also through their name and activities endorse and advance the project of erecting another national symbol, a huge statue of Christ the King, at Cerro del Cubilete, the exact geographic center of the country. Even more significantly, these years of the Guadalupanas' founding were also the years of the *Cristero* rebellion, a violent uprising in the name of the Cristo Rey against the outrages of the Ley Calles and the ensuing governmental repression. These were not merely coincidences of timing, by the way. This very specific historical context, and these (broadly speaking) political motivations, were at the heart of the community's founding; and the community's support for the *Cristero* movement and its devotion to religious liberty were explicit and heartfelt.[24]

In time, however, this very rooted Mexican identity would be wedded to the much broader designation of OSB—the Order of Saint Benedict, or Benedictine. In the very early years Mother Josefina Valencia and her small band of Misioneras Guadalupanas de

Cristo Rey labored much as Mollie Rogers and her "secretaries" had done in Ossining to find a wider congregational home and identity. Founded as an independent religious community in 1930, the group of sisters experimented with affiliation with the Carmelites and other orders in their early years before finally placing themselves in 1938 under the Rule of Saint Benedict through the influence of their cofoundress. María Placida Barrios de los Rios, looking to find a community in which she could pursue both a Benedictine monastic spirituality and a missionary apostolate, set the Guadalupanas on a very specific path that they have followed throughout their communal history.

Though the Benedictine aspect of their identity has not always been an easy affiliation for the sisters to navigate and define, they have over the course of many dynamic decades managed to establish a balance between the mission of Mother Josefina Valencia and the monastery of Mother María Placida. As a result, their apostolic work makes it impossible for the sisters to maintain the kind of traditional monastic regimen that Leo Rudloff, the abbot in Jerusalem, was so anxious to reestablish in Weston. But at the same time, the Guadalupanas have established a network of pastoral commitments and public relationships that would be impossible for a community like Weston to create. In important foundational ways, in other words, the two communities found in each other much more than a common spirit. They also found in each other very different Benedictine emphases that could, they discovered, be turned into complementary Benedictine commitments within the context of a long-term process of bringing Vermont and Mexico into intimate relationship with each other.

La Alianza

Talking to both communities at length about that relationship, as I have done over the course of several years, I cannot help but be impressed with the importance that the relationship holds for the brothers and the sisters. They speak of each other in familial terms, and the words they use to describe their ties to each other are often lyrical and poetic. In short, the brothers and sisters love each other, and they have from the very first. At that first meeting in 1976, as the brothers describe it, "something extraordinary happened. It was like a family reunion, or brothers and sisters recognizing each other for the first time."[25] For the sisters, that day was, in their words, "a gift from God."[26] One of their foundresses, Mother María Placida, had always dreamed of the sisters' connecting with Benedictine men who would treat them with respect, and here was a group of men from Vermont who did exactly that from the very first moment.[27]

"*Mucho respeto*," much respect, was the phrase I heard over and over (and over) again when I asked the sisters to explain why meeting the brothers meant so much to them. Many things impressed the sisters right away: the peaceful spirit that the brothers seemed to carry with them; the beautiful music that they shared with each other and with the sisters; the fact that they were all equal to each other in monastic solidarity; and the fact that they called each other "brother." But more than anything else, it was the simple but apparently overwhelming fact that the brothers respected the sisters— that they came to visit them, treated them as equals, and assumed that they were traveling together along the same path of Benedictine spirituality. It goes without saying, and frankly without much remark by the sisters themselves, that this was not the sort of relationship they were used to having with Benedictine men and other priests in Mexico. As the sisters emphasized to me: "To meet such informal monks was very, very unusual. We liked that they were interested in meeting us. They came looking for us; no one came looking for us. After meeting the Weston brothers, we changed. We didn't have fathers anymore. We had brothers."[28]

When I asked the brothers what it was that they loved about the sisters right away, they emphasized that they and the sisters shared the same spirit, the same openness, the same understanding of Benedictine life. That first meeting in 1976, it should be said, had to be based in spirit and openness, because it could not be based in conversation. None of the brothers spoke Spanish, and none of the sisters spoke English. All that the two groups of Benedictines could do was smile at each other and, of course, sing together. Both communities are deeply devoted to music and song as one of the central aspects of their communal life and ministry, and so that was the concrete manifestation of their shared spirit in that first meeting. They sang.

As the relationship developed and deepened over the next several years, however, it ratified the wisdom of Rembert Weakland's original insight in encouraging these two communities to find each other in the first place. Both sides benefited from their ties to each other in exactly the ways that Weakland had hoped. For the sisters, the relationship with *los hermanos* represented a powerful connection to the broader Benedictine Confederation, and to Weston's specific image of the monastic life. Starting in 1978 small groups of sisters have traveled annually to Vermont, where they join in the simplicity of the brothers' life there. On those trips they are reintroduced to the basics of Benedictine spirituality that Abbot Leo sought to place at the heart of the Priory's life in the 1950s. Prayer and work, in an environment of full equality, is how the sisters wish to define their own spiritual commitments, and Weston offers those commitments in a distilled way. And always there is the respect the brothers show them, the *mucho respeto* that still, more than thirty years later, comes as a salve in the lives of these Mexican women. "They include us in everything" is how the sisters describe their experiences in Vermont: "their prayer, work, and even their recreation. We feel privileged when we are included in the circle of the brothers of Weston."[29]

For the brothers, the relationship with "our sisters" (which is how they always refer to them) has brought related but separate benefits. In the decade or so before the brothers traveled to Mexico, they had been faced with the difficult challenge of deciding, collectively, how exactly they would relate to the world outside their hillside in Vermont. They never questioned that they would devote themselves to the reaffirmation of traditional Benedictine monasticism; they did not seriously consider adopting the pastoral work that occupies the time of many Benedictines, including the Guadalupanas. At the same time, the brothers did not desire to cut themselves off from the rest of the world entirely. Instead, in true Benedictine fashion, they wanted their monastic life to serve that world: to offer an example of consuming faithfulness, to be sure, but also to offer vaguely defined support to people and communities in their everyday struggles. For the brothers, this challenge that faces every monastic community closely intersected with the question of how they would use the considerable fame that was coming their way in response to the publication of their music. As albums like *Wherever You Go* and *Locusts and Wild Honey* became hits in Catholic circles across the United States and beyond, the brothers found themselves being drawn further and further into social and political causes that they supported but that they did not wish to make the focus of their monastic life together.

That, more than anything else, is what the Mexican sisters offered the brothers of the Weston Priory: focus. Beyond the shared spirit and *el propio carisma*, the sisters introduced the brothers to the poor people of Mexico. This connection with the poor through the sisters presented a much appreciated opportunity for the brothers to reformulate the ways in which they thought about the relationship between their community and the world outside their monastery. Through what quickly became annual visits of the entire Weston community to the sisters' *casa central* in Mexico City, and then also to the many missions the sisters maintained throughout Mexico and Central America, the brothers rapidly recognized that they "felt at home among the people of Mexico."[30] They realized, in short, that the relationship with their sisters could have three powerful effects. It could provide an external focus that would lift themselves out of the insularity inherent in being an independent conventual priory within the Benedictine Confederation. It could lead to a recommitment to Benedictine hospitality on the model so obviously provided by the sisters themselves. And finally, it could combine the first two effects by providing the Weston Priory with a mission of its own: to introduce the many music lovers and pilgrims who showed up at their doors to what the brothers came to call "the reality of the poor in Latin America." As the sisters described the shared commitment that became a central element of their *alianza*: "We are missionaries; they are monks. And we are both devoted to the poor."[31]

It can all seem so ethereal to hear them talk about each other, or indeed to visit one community or the other. They are very present in each other's homes. Pictures of the brothers are prominently displayed at the Guadalupe Center in Cuernavaca, and the music of the Weston Priory is absolutely central to the communal prayer life of the sisters both there and at the *casa central* in Mexico City. Meanwhile, the bright colors of Mexico feature prominently in the decor of the Weston Priory, and the music and dance of Mexico give the liturgical practices of the brothers a distinctly Latin American flavor. Moreover, if somehow a visitor to the monastery in Vermont was to miss the iconographic representations of the brothers' devotion to the sisters, and through them to the poor of Latin America, that visitor would not be able to miss the brothers' frequent and unmistakably genuine expression of their love for their sisters, and their appreciation for the world that the sisters have opened for them.

The relationship between these two communities is more than personal and spiritual, however. It is also deeply political (in the broadest meaning of that term), in the sense that the shared commitment to the poor of Mexico leads directly to reflection on the political, social, and economic structures within which those poor people live. But the relationship is also political in the sense that the transnational bonds between these Benedictine brothers and Benedictine sisters have led to direct action by the two communities, designed explicitly by them for the purpose of making an impact on relations (again very broadly defined) between Mexico and the United States of America. More specifically, the transnational ties between the brothers and the sisters serve as the platform on which, and from which, these Benedictine communities try to introduce *la realidad* of Mexican poverty to US citizens who are oblivious both to the existence of this poverty on their southern border and to the degree to which that reality is caused by economic and political dynamics that have their origins on the northern side of the border. As we shall see, this political project, if we can accurately use that term, is purposely intended by the brothers and sisters, is extremely diverse in its implementation, and is fundamentally grounded in the Benedictine principle of hospitality that the two communities share.

Like the Jesuits and Maryknollers we have examined in the previous chapters, these Benedictines engage in political activity in ways that are uniquely commensurate with their own internal structures and with their own communal understanding of the religious life. For the Jesuits, politics involved efforts to act *universidadamente* to change US policy toward the Salvadoran military and to get the United States to pressure the Salvadoran government to investigate and prosecute the murders at the UCA. For the Maryknollers, it was a matter of engaging in reverse mission for the purpose of raising the suffering of the people of Central America into the consciousness of voters in the United States. And for the Benedictine brothers of the Weston Priory, political activity is defined, by and large, in the indirect terms of growing closer and closer to their Benedictine sisters in Mexico and of using that relationship as the basis on which to spread a deeper awareness of the poor and suffering people whom the sisters serve throughout Latin America. In each case the transnational relationships that serve as the foundations of these communal mobilizations involve a remarkably tight weaving together of the religious with the political.

Offering Support

One of the features of this relationship on which neither the brothers nor the sisters wish to dwell is the very different levels of financial resources the two parties bring to it. Not to put too fine a point on the matter, but the brothers have made a good deal of money from their music over the years, and so they can offer substantial support to causes that they choose to support. Obviously, they support nothing as clearly and powerfully as they support their sisters and the sisters' work in Latin America, so the possibility of establishing a financial relationship existed from the very beginning. Like many relationships between relatively wealthy *gringos* and relatively less wealthy Mexicans, however, the brothers and the sisters had to struggle at first to figure out what role US dollars would play in their relationship and, frankly, to figure out how they could build their relationship on something deeper and more mutually beneficial than charity.[32]

This is not to say that money does not change hands, or that the brothers do not financially support the work of the sisters. I had the distinct impression in interacting with both communities that there is a financial component to the relationship. But beyond the mutual benefits I have already noted, ones that are based on shared commitments and communal solidarity, the brothers do offer the sisters and their work a level of support that goes well beyond finances. In a word, they provide the sisters with a level of access to levers of power in the US government that a group of Catholic nuns in Mexico City could never hope to establish on their own. Like Donald Monan in regards to El Salvador, or Peggy Healy in the case of Nicaragua, the brothers of the Weston Priory are prominent US citizens who are well positioned to bring pressure to bear on US officials in ways that can at times prove powerfully beneficial to the sisters in Mexico and to the poor people with whom the sisters work.

Margaret Keck and Kathryn Sikkink, in their book on transnational advocacy networks, wrote of a "boomerang effect," whereby "domestic NGOs bypass their states and directly search out international allies to try to bring pressure on their states from outside."[33] This definition clearly applies to the efforts by Jesuits based in the United States to turn their influence in the US Congress not only into pressure on the US administration to alter policy towards El Salvador, but also indirectly into pressure on the Salvadoran government to intensify its efforts to solve the murders at the UCA. But the definition applies even more clearly here in the case of the transnational network of communication and support between Vermont and Mexico. The Benedictine sisters have no local political influence that would allow them to appeal to their own government in Mexico. And so they turn to their *hermanos* outside of Mexico, the monks of the Weston Priory, who can powerfully influence events in Mexico: not through direct engagement with the Mexican government, but rather indirectly through engagement with their friends in the US government. The fact is that the brothers are rather prominent Vermonters who have long-standing personal and political ties to political figures like Senator Pat Leahy (D-VT) and Senator Bernie Sanders (I-VT). It is these relationships in the United States that "boomerang" to the sisters' benefit in Mexico. The sisters inform the brothers, who ask for help from their senators, who make requests to the State Department, which intervenes with the Mexican government.

The sisters like to tell the story of a land dispute involving a group of their people in Oaxaca, Mexico, that was solved (miraculously, it seemed to them) by the intervention of the brothers through their congressional representatives in Vermont. The brothers also celebrate this particular case of boomerang intervention, and they speak of it with some humble pride. At the same time, the brothers point out that this case in Oaxaca is just one case of many, one example when they were able to ask their friends in Washington to help their friends in Mexico. The brothers stress the element of friendship in these interactions; and they emphasize that when they ask, say, Leahy or Sanders to act on behalf of people in Mexico, they are asking on behalf of places the brothers have actually been, and on behalf of people they actually know. They are asking their senators, in short, to help them help their friends in Mexico, the people and circumstances that the sisters have introduced them to. It is easy to see why this kind of personalized politics is so attractive to the brothers of the Weston Priory. It is one thing to sing at a political protest or write letters on behalf of a distant cause. It is entirely another thing to advocate on behalf of people you personally know, especially if they are people to whom your Benedictine sisters have devoted their lives.

Sanctuary

Because the Rule of Saint Benedict requires of all Benedictine communities that "any guest who happens to arrive at the monastery should be received just as . . . Christ himself," hospitality resides at the very core of Benedictine practice and spirituality.[34] As I mentioned at the beginning of this chapter, a (relatively) open door is a pervasive commitment in the Benedictine world, certainly so at the priory in Weston, the motherhouse in Mexico City, and the Guadalupe Center in Cuernavaca. The two communities, in addition to walking together into a shared future with confident trust in the face of its uncertainty, also work together to welcome guests as if they were Christ. That being the case, it is difficult to think of a public issue more likely to capture the attention of the Benedictine brothers and sisters than the plight of refugees fleeing civil strife in Central America during the 1970s and 1980s.

The Guadalupanas were deeply involved in the early 1980s in ferrying Salvadorans and Guatemalans through Mexico to safety in the United States of America, and it was a natural thing for them to invite the monks from Weston to join them in that effort. Earlier chapters of this book have touched on the brutal conditions that existed in Central America in those years, and on the many thousands of people who were put at risk by the civil wars that raged in their midst. Many of those in particular danger were Salvadorans and Guatemalans who were working with local church officials and groups to respond to the plight of the poor in those societies. The kind of people for whom Ignacio Ellacuría spoke in El Salvador, for whom the Melvilles struggled in Guatemala, and for whom Nancy Donovan wept in Nicaragua were offered safe haven by people like the sisters in Mexico City, and sanctuary by the brothers in Vermont.

"Sanctuary," in fact, was the name given a movement among Christian churches to defy Immigration and Naturalization Services (INS) policy on Central American refugees/migrants by engineering unsanctioned entry into the United States for people fleeing persecution in El Salvador and Guatemala, and then by offering those migrants shelter and support once they had arrived in the United States. The movement began rather informally in Arizona in 1981 when two men, John Fife and Jim Corbett, stumbled into the practice of rescuing refugees from border patrol agents and the INS bureaucracy and asking local church communities to provide sanctuary for them.[35] The idea behind the movement was the assumption that the US government would be less likely to raid an actual church building than individual houses, and the movement was based in a very old Christian tradition of turning agents of the state back from church doors. Tellingly referring to the movement as a "ministry of hospitality" in his book *This Ground Is Holy: Church Sanctuary and Central American Refugees*, Ignatius Bau offered two quotations that revealed the motives at the heart of the sanctuary movement.[36] The first quoted a pastor of a church in Chicago, a member of the

Chicago Religious Task Force on Central America, and it is dated 1982: "We provide a safe place and cry 'Basta! Enough! The blood stops here at our doors.' This is the time to claim our sacred right to invoke the name of God in this place—to push back all the powers of violation and violence in the name of the Spirit to whom we owe our ultimate allegiance. At this historic moment we are the people to tell Caesar, 'no trespassing, for the ground upon which you walk is holy.'"[37]

Bau's second passage quoted Eric Jorsted from a contemporaneous article he published in the *Christian Century* magazine: "Sanctuary is first an act of compassion, an expression of the fundamental Christian concern to love one's neighbor . . . sanctuary is a way of expressing compassion in caring for our suffering neighbors from Central America. It is a way of providing for people in need, not only with social services, but also by giving them haven from potentially disastrous consequences of deportation."[38]

The movement started small. But soon it spread from Arizona across the country, and hundreds of churches became involved in sheltering thousands of refugees. And on March 24, 1984—significantly, the fourth anniversary of the murder of Oscar Romero in San Salvador—the Weston Priory formally became a place of sanctuary when the brothers welcomed from Guatemala the family of Felipe and Elena Ixcot and their five children.[39] Bau made the point in *This Ground Is Holy* that many churches in this period had a difficult time integrating their commitment to sanctuary with the rest of the commitments and activities they carried out as religious communities. In many cases it was awkward to have persons—persons who risked arrest if they left the grounds—actually living in church buildings. Because of these complicating factors, some churches became what Bau called "secondary sanctuaries," or communities that offered support and protection to refugees who were actually housed in secret elsewhere.[40] The monks of the Weston Priory, however, were able to commit their monastery to being an "immediate sanctuary," and they did so in the knowledge that the Ixcots would not detract from the growing mission of the monastic community; to the contrary, they would embody it.[41] The family could actually live on the grounds of the priory (the Ixcots, in fact, raised their family on the grounds of the priory and did not return to Guatemala for good until twenty-five years later, in 2009), and in so doing they could not only enjoy the safety of the brothers' sanctuary but could also serve as a tangible sign of the brothers' broader desire to extend hospitality and support to the poor people of Latin America.

Not at all surprisingly, the inspiration for offering the Weston Priory as a sanctuary to Central American refugees came from the Misioneras Guadalupanas de Cristo Rey in Mexico. The process began in February 1983 when the sisters invited a group of visiting brothers to accompany them to a village in southern Mexico, where they could meet and hear the story of a family who had fled violence in Guatemala. This arrangement was quite typical of the relationship between the brothers and the sisters at that time. Brothers would come to visit Mexico—first in small groups, and later as a whole community—and the sisters would involve the brothers in their work primarily by taking them around to missions to introduce the brothers to the people with whom and for whom the sisters worked. This was the primary method through which the brothers were introduced to what they refer to as the "reality" of Latin America, and this particular trip in 1983 had a particularly profound effect on the five brothers who met the Guatemalan family.

One of those five brothers later described in the priory's newsletter how one of the family's older children "anxiously rises from time to time to look cautiously out of the window—an opening in the block concrete wall—to see if anyone is listening to the subdued conversation within. [A] woman's quiet voice is filled with feeling," he wrote, as she described the world of death and fear that she and her family had left behind in Guatemala and appealed to the visiting North Americans to do something, anything, to help them and the many people like them. "Brothers," she implored, "tell your people that we are not Communists—we are simple people, Christians like yourselves, who only want food and shelter for our families, a place to work and live. Please, brothers, tell your people to stop your government from sending more arms that only kill and hurt our people."[42]

In many ways the reaction that the brothers had to this testimony and request was very similar to the reaction that Peggy Healy and Nancy Donovan had to the suffering of the people (*their* people) during the United States–supported contra war in Nicaragua. "There is genocide going on in Latin America," the monk from Weston wrote a month after the clandestine meeting in Mexico. "Our own government is supplying advisors, bombs, planes, spare parts—all being used to exterminate a people. Weapons made by our hands, paid for with our money. Our government is telling us that it is doing it for the good of our country."[43] The Maryknoll sisters confronted the same dynamic among the people with whom they lived along the Honduran border in Nicaragua. When Donovan and Healy saw what *their* government was doing to *their* people, they did what their missionary community was structured and devoted to doing: They sought to evangelize the people of the United States through the process of reverse mission. They came home to the United States and traveled around telling people what was happening in their name in Central America.

We will see in a moment that the brothers of the Weston Priory also sought to use their particular notoriety as a platform from which to educate their compatriots—or at least their fellow Vermonters—about what was happening so many miles to the south. But the brothers are not missionaries. They are monks, devoted to Leo Rudloff's vision of a traditional monastic life centered on prayer and work, rather than pastoral outreach. So when filled with their own outrage at what was being done in their name, the brothers responded in a monastic way, through methods deeply ingrained in their Benedictine tradition. They prayed, of course. Everything is structured around prayer in Weston, and as the Rule says, prayer is "the first step of anything worthwhile."[44] But the brothers also moved readily to a decision to offer hospitality to some of the suffering people about whom they had learned through the work of the sisters. When the five brothers returned from Mexico in 1983, they contacted the Chicago Religious Task Force on Central America, and they offered their monastic home as a sanctuary to Guatemalan refugees. And when they did, they also acknowledged, as they always do, the crucial role that the sisters in Mexico had played in leading them to their decision:

On March 24, 1984, the fourth anniversary of the assassination of Archbishop Oscar Arnulfo Romero in El Salvador, we opened the doors of our monastery to welcome a family of refugees from Guatemala who were fleeing from repression and death in their country. We declared Weston Priory a Public Sanctuary for Central American refugees. . . . In our choice to offer Public Sanctuary, we continued a journey that had begun with our Mexican Benedictine sisters. Through the sisters, we encountered the suffering and hope of the poorest people of Latin America—including that of refugees fleeing the brutality of military governments in Central America."[45]

Vamos!

In addition to their own travels to Mexico and their own involvement in the sanctuary movement, the brothers of the Weston Priory were indeed able to carry out their own form of reverse mission by speaking about their experiences with the many, many people with whom they interact in Vermont and across the United States. As I have alluded to a couple of times already, the monks are celebrities of a sort for a certain segment of the Catholic population in the United States. The brothers resist that status, and they are constantly seeking to express humility and solidarity within the framework of their fame. But regardless, they *are* famous. And that fame, and the music on which it is based, brings large crowds of people to the hillside in Vermont to hear the brothers' music, to experience for an hour, a day, or a week the rhythms of their monastic life—and to hear the brothers speak often and passionately about their sisters in Mexico and about *la realidad* that the sisters have introduced them to. Mexican music, Mexican dance, and frequent visits by Mexican nuns all lend a pervasive sense of mission and transnational solidarity to the iconography and activities of the Weston Priory, and they do not go unnoticed by the many guests. At the same time, the brothers publish a newsletter twice a year and maintain a lively website that, in addition to offering their music and handicrafts for sale, provides a very detailed account of the community's activities, commitments, and priorities. To say that the Mexican sisters and the

Arco Iris de Alianza occupy a prominent place in these narratives would be to understate the degree to which the brothers present themselves publicly, in all of their available forums, as devoted to the Alianza, to their sisters, and to the poor people of Latin America with whom the sisters work.

In my many conversations with them, the brothers did not evince much concern as to the practical ramifications of all of this education and, in a way, evangelization in Vermont.[46] As one might expect from men who have been living a life of relative solitude and silence for decades, they tend to take a long view of developments, and they tend to calmly accept the complex ways in which words, experiences, and political change all come to influence together. In short, the brothers do not speak of their sisters with the idea that their listeners will be transformed utterly or act immediately. Instead, they seek to share their experiences in Latin America with those who come to hear their music and share their hospitality, in the hope that they will be able to make some indirect but tangible impact on the level of understanding and solidarity that will exist in the future across the United States–Mexico border.

This is not to say, however, that the brothers' efforts to transport the reality of Mexico and Latin America to Vermont and the United States have not had practical, tangible effects. They have—and none more tangible or practical, though typically indirect, than the establishment of Vamos!, a sprawling network of Mexican community centers and social service outposts headquartered, predictably enough, in Weston, Vermont, and Cuernavaca, Mexico. Vamos! is actually the brainchild and life's work of William and Patty Coleman, two residents of Weston who came to know the brothers and their connection to Mexico through frequent visits to the priory. The Colemans became such trusted friends that they were sent by the monks to meet some of the sisters in Cuernavaca and to become familiar with the sisters' work there with the poor. Like many visitors to the City of Eternal Spring, the Colemans were heartbroken by the people they encountered in Mexico, particularly by the children who roamed the streets all day selling gum or trinkets and who showed no signs of having homes, schools, or communities who would care for them. Unlike most visitors, however, the Colemans decided to do much more than buy a poncho or some jewelry at the zocalo in Cuernavaca and then return home with a somewhat heavier heart. Instead, the Colemans decided to move to Cuernavaca and dedicate themselves to providing safe places where those children, and their families, could receive at least some minimal level of physical, emotional, and spiritual support.

In 1987 the Colemans started Vamos!, an organization that now supports about a dozen community centers in Cuernavaca and the surrounding villages.[47] Funded by individual contributions, and supported by many volunteers who travel from the United States for anywhere from a few days to a couple of years, Vamos! is a fiercely independent entity that trumpets in its literature that it "receives no governmental or institutional support" and that "every cent you donate goes to the Mexican poor." I had the opportunity to visit Vamos! in January 2009, and what I found at Casa Tatic in Cuernavaca was a bustling community center in which every room was filled with either small children doing arts and crafts and other preschool-like activities, or young women engaged in what can best be described as parenting classes or in the work of a sewing cooperative that produces shirts and shawls for sale in the open-air markets that dot the city. Across the street was Casa Romero, a lovely little building filled with colorful artworks and crafts, all produced and sold by the artisan cooperative that Vamos! established to keep artists and their children off the street. As the website puts it, Casa Tatic is a place where more than 250 people come each day to "study, play, sing, dance, brush their teeth, take their vitamins, and most important, eat." Yes, eat—because perhaps more than anything else, the centers associated with Vamos! are dedicated to providing nutritious meals for people, especially children, who spend up to twelve hours a day on the streets hawking goods to tourists. Casa Tatic alone claims to provide more than twenty thousand meals a year to these children.

It is important to emphasize again that Vamos! is not a pastoral activity of the brothers of the Weston Priory. In fact, the brothers do not have anything to do with Vamos! on a day-to-day basis. It was and remains a separate project, founded by the Colemans and maintained through the work of paid staff and volunteers who are not directly affiliated with the priory. But direct affiliation is not the point I am trying to emphasize here. The point, rather, is that the relationship between the brothers and sisters, the transnational Benedictine network that the two communities established decades ago, has had implications and ramifications well beyond the priory in Vermont and the motherhouse in Mexico. That relationship has introduced friends of the brothers to their sisters in Mexico, and it has led to the establishment of close connections between Vermont and Mexico that are all modeled on the Benedictine commitment to hospitality. In the case of Vamos!, people from Vermont went and found the needy and moved in next door to them (as the Maryknoll sister in San Salvador put it). The Colemans left the priory and Vermont and moved to Mexico so that they could provide hospitality where it was most needed. But the hospitality they offer at Casa Tatic and throughout the Vamos! network is based on the same Benedictine principle of greeting the guest—in this case a homeless child—as one would greet Christ himself.

There are still close, though informal ties, between the priory and Vamos!, by the way. For one thing, the sisters at the Guadalupe Center make a point of bringing all of their guests from the United States to Casa Tatic so that their guests can learn about the services that Vamos! provides and support the program by buying the handiworks that are for sale across the street at Casa Romero. Moreover, many of the volunteers and contributors who support Vamos! do so after learning about the program and its activities during visits to the Weston Priory to meet the brothers and hear them sing. There is a thriving community of people who meet each other at the priory, both in a physical sense and in symbolic terms, and that community has made a close connection with the people of Cuernavaca through the brothers and through Vamos! And perhaps most symbolically and most significantly for my purposes in this chapter, when Vamos! celebrated in September 2007 its twentieth anniversary in operation, the celebration was held at the place where the program found its first inspiration, and where the Colemans were first introduced to *la realidad* of Mexico. The party was held a couple of thousand miles north from Cuernavaca, on the grounds of the Weston Priory in rural Vermont.

Extending the Network

The brothers' interaction with Latin America has also, thanks to the sisters, extended well beyond Mexico itself. The Guadalupanas now have missions and houses in Nicaragua and Guatemala as well, so of course the Weston monks have visited these outposts and related their experiences there to the many US citizens who visit them at Weston or read about their travels in their publications. At the same time, the sisters in Mexico have made a point of introducing their brothers to still other Benedictine communities in the region, both within Mexico itself and also as far away as central Brazil. None of these other communal connections or relationships has yet taken on nearly the intimacy or significance of the Arco Iris de Alianza. But it is nevertheless true to say that the Alianza has served as the basic foundation for what has now become a rather extended trans-national network of like-minded Benedictine communities in the Western hemisphere.

Of all the trips the brothers have taken throughout Latin America with the sisters, however, none have been as politically charged as the two visits the monks made to Nicaragua, the first in 1988, and the second thirteen years later in 2001. The brothers declared the purpose of their first visit to Managua in 1988 as an opportunity "to express solidarity and hope to the poor and suffering people of Nicaragua" and "to be a monastic witness of conscience to our fellow citizens of the United States."[48] It is important to point out that this visit occurred when the US government was deeply involved in supporting (some would say instigating) the contra war against the Sandinista government of Nicaragua, and at a time when this matter was the subject of sharp political contestation within the United States. This was the same war, and the same US foreign policy, that had so inflamed Maryknoll sisters like Nancy Donovan and Peggy Healy that they had been moved to return from the mission field and travel across the United States arguing against the US policy and asking their fellow citizens to rise in opposition to it.

The monks of the Weston Priory launched no such concerted effort and committed themselves to no such speaking tour. That would definitely not be part of their monastic style. But the monks did feel the same kind of outrage that had moved the Maryknollers, and they expressed that outrage sharply to any and all who would listen: US embassy officials in Managua, congressional representatives in Vermont, and the many people who attended their services at Weston and read their publications. In fact, the brothers' description of their trip to Nicaragua (accompanied by four Mexican sisters, of course) and their own reaction to it walked the same tenuous line that Maryknollers like Nancy Donovan had walked between angry opposition to the contra war (which was a controversial political position to take at the time) and actual support for the Sandinista regime itself (which would have been a *very* controversial position to take at the time).

Consider, for example, the tone of approbation that the brothers adopted in describing a factory they visited where the women who worked the sewing machines also held an ownership stake in the enterprise itself. The women, the Weston newsletter reported, "are positive about being more in control of their own lives, about the hours they work, the spirit of cooperation, and the sharing in decision-making and ownership." Or consider also the tone of saddened outrage with which they described the innocent victims of the contra war whom they encountered at a children's hospital, populated by youngsters who stepped on landmines. Even a Sandinista prison was described in the newsletter as a place of relative dignity, where "the exchange between prisoners and guards is remarkable for its sense of mutual respect." Summing up their trip to Nicaragua in 1988, the brothers admitted, "In the short time we have in Nicaragua it is clear that we brothers and sisters will not get to see the full reality. But," they nevertheless concluded, "we are being shown areas that give us a taste of what this dream might become."[49]

This dream? To what does this phrase refer? In context it is clear that it refers to the policy program of expanded educational opportunities, universal access to health care facilities, and targeted attention to the needs of the poor that was presented by the Sandinista president Daniel Ortega at a public speech in Managua attended by the brothers from Vermont and the sisters from Mexico. Again, the key thing to keep in mind in assessing the import of the brothers' very favorable narrative is the political context in which it was offered. This was 1988; Ronald Reagan was still president of the United States. The Sandinistas were being roundly condemned by his administration as a communist beachhead in America's backyard, and the contras were being lionized as "the moral equal to our Founding Fathers."[50] To the middle-class Roman Catholics who made up most of the monks' audience back in Weston and beyond, the monks' words would have directly contradicted what they were hearing from their own national government and largely from their own national media.

The tone of hopeful praise that characterized the account of the 1988 trip is even more pronounced when considered in juxtaposition to the baleful tone that the brothers adopted in describing what they called their "very different journey" to post-Sandinista Nicaragua in 2001.[51] While the Managua of 1988 was described as a bustling metropolis of industrious revolutionaries ("No beggars!"), the city that the brothers returned to thirteen years later was said to be filled with sad-eyed children holding one hand out to walk along the streets with the brothers, and holding the other hand out to ask them for money. Gone are the hopeful passages about owner-workers and respectful prisoners, and in their place is the summation remark that "the Sandinistas are no longer in power, and the corruption of the current government is comparable to that of the Somoza regime."[52]

From the very beginning, however, this second trip in 2001 was far less obviously political than the first, in the way that "political" is usually meant. This time, for example, there were no tense sessions with US embassy officials at which the brothers would express their stark opposition to US policy in terms of Christian morality. By 2001 the Benedictine sisters had established two missions of their own in Nicaragua—one in Managua and one in the countryside—so the second trip was also more personal in that sense than the first. Whereas the monks had merely been accompanied by four of their sisters in 1988, this time they were actually visiting their sisters, experiencing their hospitality, and expressing their own solidarity with and support for the sisters' work with the poorest of the poor in Nicaraguan society. Even more specifically and personally, the brothers in conjunction with the sisters had organized a fundraising drive to support people in Nicaragua whose homes and lives had been devastated by Hurricane Mitch a few years earlier. The brothers had channeled those funds to the people through the Mexican (and now Nicaraguan) sisters, of course, so the brothers had traveled to Nicaragua at the sisters' invitation to see how the money was being spent, and to remind themselves of the profound needs that remained among the people.

In that sense the trip to Nicaragua in 2001 was very similar to a trip the brothers took to Guatemala in 2003. In this case the monks traveled from Weston to the Monasterio Reina de Paz, a monastery that the Guadalupanas had taken possession of shortly before, and they observed the work that the sisters were doing with the poor people in and around the city of Cobán, Guatemala. Again, the brothers' reports on their travels were filled with humble awe at the sisters' presence with the poor of Guatemala, and they made passionate pleas that their listeners and readers "open their hearts" to the suffering peoples of Latin America. This time, however, there was an even more personal connection to Guatemala, because Felipe and Elena Ixcot were visiting their homeland at the same time that the brothers visited the sisters. The Ixcots and the brothers were able to spend time together in Cobán during this visit, and so the Guatemalan couple who had been living in sanctuary at the Weston Priory for more than twenty years by that time could share with the monks the pride they felt in the midwife center that they had helped to bring into being in their hometown of Concepción Chiquirichapa.[53]

In short, the lines of intersection and connection in this particular transnational network of religious community have grown remarkably complex and mutually reinforcing over the years. The brothers from Vermont met the sisters from Mexico in 1976, and from that first meeting they developed a relationship, an *alianza*, of unique depth and closeness. That relationship led to frequent cross-border interaction between the two communities, but it also led to US senators from Vermont advocating on behalf of landless peasants in Oaxaca, to Vamos! establishing a network of community centers and health clinics in and around Cuernavaca, to the brothers traveling to Nicaragua to witness in opposition to US policy there, to devotees of the monks' music raising money to aid victims of Hurricane Mitch, to the priory itself being declared a public sanctuary for Central American refugees, and to those very refugees organizing (from Vermont) a midwife center in their tiny home village in Guatemala. All of it, as I have emphasized throughout this chapter, was paradigmatically transnational, in the sense that analysts of international relations use that term—but all of it was also distinctively Benedictine, in that it was structured through community and grounded in hospitality.

One other branch of this transnational network is worthy of note, particularly for the degree to which it actually came to shape the membership of the monastery at Weston itself. In the spring of 2002 the brothers traveled at the invitation of the Mexican sisters to Goias, Brazil, to meet and spend time with the monks of the Benedictine Monastery of the Annunciation of the Lord.[54] There, as usual, the monks from Vermont walked the streets of the local *barrios*, interacted with the poor people who lived near the monastery, and visited some of the centers of social outreach that the Brazilian brothers had established in the vicinity. And also as usual, the monks from Weston reported back to their friends in Vermont and the United States about how their lives had been affected and their hearts opened by their experience in Brazil. In this case, however, the creation of transnational community was even more obvious and tangible than usual. For one thing, the monastery in Goias (oddly enough, for those not familiar with Benedictine structures) is actually a foundation of the Benedictine Abbey of Tournay in the south of France, and it is overseen by a Frenchman named Joel Chauvelot. More important to the monks from Weston, however, is that while in Goias they made the acquaintance of a Brazilian man who was staying at the Annunciation monastery while he was considering committing himself to the monastic life. Impressed with the spirit of openness and brotherhood he observed among the Vermonters, however, this Brazilian man soon traveled to Weston himself, where he joined the monastic community and where in short order he became a fully professed member of the Weston Priory. In fact, this particular brother was not the first man who had come to the priory directly through the relationship with the sisters. A number of years earlier the sisters had introduced the brothers to another future monk, in this case a Mexican who had been taught as a young man by some of the Guadalupanas at a school in Mexico City. The presence of these two brothers in Vermont indicates that the transnational monastic ties between the United States and Latin America that Rembert Weakland had originally hoped to forge had come to fruition in a tangible way that was for the brothers both deeply personal and absolutely fundamental to the structure of their communal life. In short, the *alianza* with the sisters in Mexico not only had transformed the mission of the Weston Priory but had also reshaped the very nature of the priory's brotherhood itself.

The Guadalupe Center

All of these implications of the relationship between the brothers and the sisters pale, however, in comparison to the value they all place on the Guadalupe Center in Cuernavaca. In an important sense, the Alianza itself was created first for the purpose of establishing a solid communal foundation on which a shared space could be constructed and occupied by the brothers of the Weston Priory and the Misioneras Guadalupanas de Cristo Rey. It took several years to pick out the site and construct the facilities in Cuernavaca; but once the center opened in 1984, it served two absolutely crucial purposes.[55] The first was that it served as the brothers' home away from home in Mexico, a consistent place where they could go on their annual visits to reconnect with the sisters and renew their acquaintance with the work that the sisters perform among the poor in Latin America. But the second was that, for most of the year, the Guadalupe Center serves as the site of a program called the Faith and Hospitality Experience in a Latin American Context, during which "the sisters seek to introduce participants to the present-day reality of the Mexican people and to give some understanding of life and faith lived in Latin America."[56] This ten-day experience, held roughly ten times a year for roughly fifteen visitors at a time, is part religious retreat, part political seminar, and part anthropological fieldwork.

The program in Mexico is run entirely by the sisters, about ten of whom actually live and work at the Guadalupe Center in Cuernavaca. But all the advertising of the experience and all the arrangements for participation are handled directly through the Weston Priory in Vermont. Moreover, the brothers, who are never actually in Mexico when visitors are staying at the center, are nevertheless quite present in the Faith and Hospitality Experience, both in spirit and in song. The music from Weston serves as a kind of spiritual background for the prayerful Benedictine atmosphere that the sisters work so diligently to set at the Guadalupe Center. And the purposes for which the brothers sought to establish the center—their desire to share with others "the warm hospitality and the vital faith of the Mexican people in the prayerful context of the sisters' dedicated work with the poor . . . of Mexico" infuses every second of the experience.[57]

But so does the political purpose for which the Guadalupe Center was established. Again using the term "political" in its broadest meaning, the experience in Cuernavaca is unmistakably designed by the brothers and sisters to advance the political goal of introducing visitors, "especially persons from the United States and Canada," to the extent to which poverty and suffering define the life of millions of Mexicans, and it is intended to encourage those visitors to recognize the pernicious role that US foreign policy has played in perpetuating that suffering. I attended the Faith and Hospitality Experience in Cuernavaca in January 2009 as both a participant and an observer, and I was continually impressed by the strength and clarity of the political messages being conveyed by the sisters to their visitors. Yes, it was all distinctly Benedictine in style and purpose, in the sense that the sisters seemed more intent on converting hearts than on mobilizing votes. But it would be impossible to spend ten days at the Guadalupe Center in Cuernavaca and not come away with the very clear impression that the Misioneras Guadalupanas de Cristo Rey and their brothers of the Weston Priory strongly oppose the North American Free Trade Agreement (NAFTA), the International Monetary Fund, and all neoliberal international economic policies. And it would be equally impossible not to recognize that they want their guests to conclude that it is those guests' personal responsibility as Christians—US Christians, implicated in political and economic structures that are deeply harmful to the poor of Latin America—to oppose those policies as well.

The experience begins when participants are collected at the airport in Mexico City and are driven to the sisters' *casa central*, which sits along a side street only three blocks from the Basilica of Our Lady of Guadalupe. The basilica is, of course, the holiest shrine in Mexican Catholicism. It is built near the site where the Virgin of Guadalupe is said to have appeared to Juan Diego in 1531, and it still houses the cloak that ostensibly bears the indelible mark of the Virgin's physical presence in Mexico. Millions of pilgrims visit the shrine each year to worship in the basilica and the several other churches that make up the compound, to climb the actual hillside where the apparition is said to have occurred, and to glide by the sacred cloak on the moving walkway that was installed to keep the constant stream of believers and curiosity-seekers from clogging the pathway. A visit to the basilica with several sisters is the highlight of the first day of the experience in Mexico City, but it comes only after a heartfelt presentation at the *casa central* on the Virgin of Guadalupe and her powerful meaning to the Mexican people.

The first thing that struck me about the filmstrip that served as the source material for the presentation was that it was narrated by brothers of the Weston Priory. None of the other members of my group were aware of that fact, I am sure, but the sisters in the room certainly appreciated my surprised smile of recognition. What the brothers narrated (and acted out in voice), and what the sisters passionately commented on, was a version of the Guadalupe myth deeply infused with the notion that the Virgin had appeared to an indigenous peasant—rather than to a bishop, say, or to a member of the Spanish elite—in order to send a clear and ringing signal that God had special concern for the poor and the powerless. By appearing to that man in that setting, the sisters (and the voices of the brothers) emphasized, the patroness of the Mexican people was giving *mucho respeto* to the indigenous people and saying that "God is with the humble and not with the oppressor." We were told by the sisters that "through Juan Diego, Mary wants dignity to be given back to the poor, and for the poor to occupy their rightful place in society." And the presentation ended with one of the sisters declaring, "For us to believe in the Virgin of Guadalupe is also to believe in Juan Diego and all he represents."[58]

After just one day in Mexico City, one of the younger sisters drives the visitors to the Guadalupe Center in Cuernavaca, where the experience in faith and hospitality really begins in full. A packed van pulls onto the lush and beautiful grounds of the center; and as each visitor emerges from the van to be greeted by the sisters, he or she is enveloped in a series of warm hugs, punctuated by heartfelt exclamations of "Welcome home!" Hospitality, indeed . . . a central theme that was reinforced by the handwritten card of welcome on the table of each individual room, a card that in my case read "Welcome Home Timothy Byrnes." The other themes of the experience were equally clear right from the start, however, and they were just as powerfully expressed in the readings that the sisters chose for the first communal prayer service that was held on the first day in Cuernavaca. After setting the mood by playing a CD of two songs by the Weston monks (whose picture was prominently displayed at the center), the sisters had two of their visitors read aloud the spiritual readings for the day. The first was a gospel story of Jesus healing a leper, and the second was a selection from Jon Sobrino, a prominent scholar of liberation theology, and a Jesuit resident of the UCA in El Salvador whose life was spared by the pure coincidence that he was away from home on the night of the murders. The Sobrino reading argued that miracles such as the healings described in the Gospel were to be interpreted as signs of the reality of God's kingdom and of the real possibility of liberation in Christ Jesus.

As I have said, there are many purposes to the Faith and Hospitality Experience in Mexico, and converting the hearts of its participants is certainly the one that is emphasized most explicitly by the brothers and sisters who organize it. But these opening events—the first concerning Juan Diego in Mexico City, and the second involving the words of Jon Sobrino in Cuernavaca—set a very clear tone for all of the many experiences that were provided by the sisters over the course of the ensuing ten days of my experience there. Whether one is touring the community centers built by Vamos!, meeting with local sewing cooperatives and Christian base communities, visiting an orphanage, or just stopping for a visit at the home of a local woman about to be evicted by the government from her very humble but much loved home of thirty-five years, the consistent message is unmistakable: Poverty is neither an inevitable element of human existence nor an intended function of God's will. To the contrary, millions of Mexicans are destitute not because God wills them to be poor, but rather because policies pursued in Washington and other centers of international power and capital consign them to be so. Poverty, according to this argument, is a preventable tragedy that is the explicit result of the sinful structures that enrich the north at the direct expense of the south.

What I would call the experiential message of the outings in and around Cuernavaca is powerfully reinforced by the three central activities that take place at the Guadalupe Center itself. The first is a series of daily lectures by local academics and activists who emphasize the horrors visited on the Mexican poor by NAFTA and by the general approach to north-south economic relations that has defined US policy towards Mexico for as long as anyone can remember. The second is the nightly discussions during which the sisters and their visitors reflect on what they have experienced that day and how those experiences conform with their understanding of justice and of the dictates of Christian teaching. And the third central activity is the calming rhythms of the Benedictine schedule that is kept by the sisters and is participated in by their guests as a central element of the experience itself. *Ora* is represented by the communal prayer services held several times a day in the center's chapel; and *labora* by the kitchen duties that participants perform with the sisters after each meal.

As a result of this very effective combination of activities, the social, economic, and political messages of the experience are deeply embedded in the palpable warmth of the sisters' hospitality. As the brothers wished when they first had the dream of sharing their sisters' hospitality with other persons, particularly from the United States and Canada, people who travel to Mexico for the Faith and Hospitality Experience in a Latin American Context generally return to their homes with a deep sense of the degree to which their Christian faith (and I assume most of the participants are people of faith when they arrive) ought to drive them to have a change of heart concerning the relationship between their relative wealth in the north and the relative poverty of their brothers and sisters in the south. This change of heart is meant only to be launched in Mexico through a limited but direct experience of the structures of Benedictine community, spirituality, and hospitality, and through an equally limited introduction to *la realidad* within which the sisters live and work. The hope, however, is for that change of heart to take root back in the United States and to create a community of people who will share the brothers' sense of connectedness with the sisters, and who will do something—anything—to bring about change in the structures that perpetuate the suffering of the people among whom the Guadalupanas live in Mexico and throughout Latin America.

Conclusion

A central claim of this book is that each of the three religious communities under examination—the Society of Jesus, the mission society of Maryknoll, and the Benedictine Confederation—all construct their transnational ties, and the political activities that result from those ties, according to the institutional structures and communal commitments that most fundamentally define the nature of the individual communities themselves. We saw that to be true over the course of the two other case studies in earlier chapters, but the influence of communal structure and congregational commitment may be even clearer and more powerful in this case than it was in the context of the Jesuits and the Maryknollers. The Faith and Hospitality Experience in the Guadalupe Center, for example, is embedded in a very direct way in the monastic silence, communal prayer, and enveloping hospitality that every one of these particular men and women would tell you is the very definition of their own lives as Benedictine monastics.

I have to admit that I had a number of what I might call academic qualms about the Faith and Hospitality Experience I had in Mexico. Given the unavoidable time constraints of a ten-day schedule, there is no way around the fact that the program will be necessarily incomplete and in some ways superficial. The problem is that this very superficiality, as any experienced anthropologist will tell you, holds the potential within it of a number of unfortunate dynamics. At worst, a passing introduction to what the program's website calls "the present human reality of the people" at a "poor squatter settlement near the center [and] a mission area on the edge of the city" can amount, for some people, to little more than a form of poverty tourism that would be at its heart exploitative of the poor people visited during the experience. At best, one might question the relatively obvious commercial stake that many of the people who were visited had in their interaction with the visitors— nearly every person I met during my stay was primed to sell me something or other, and all were equally willing to tell me how valuable my money could be in helping them to endure their condition. In voicing these qualms, I do not mean to impugn the motives of the brothers and sisters who offer the experience to so many visitors. In personal terms I was deeply impressed with the obvious care that the sisters showed to the people we visited, and like the brothers I was inspired by the sisters' palpable commitment to live with and serve the poorest of the poor. I only mention these other possible interpretations of the experience by way of cautioning about the difficulty of actually recreating transnational relationships and Benedictine solidarity in such a short period of time.

In contrast to the unavoidable limitations of the ten-day experience, however, the brothers themselves have embarked, as they describe it, on a journey of over three decades' duration, through which they have grown ever more intimately involved with their sisters in Mexico, and ever more passionately committed to expanding that relationship to build a broader understanding within the United States of the Latin American reality. This is obviously an ambitious goal, but what makes it so interesting and so appropriate to the broader goals of this book is that the goal is pursued so clearly in ways appropriate to the brothers' Benedictine ethos, ways consistent with their monastic commitments. Yes, the monks declared the priory to be a public sanctuary for Central American refugees, and yes, they frequently contact their local and national representatives to advocate one course of policy or another. But compared to, say, the Jesuit university presidents we examined in chapter 2, or the Maryknoll sisters we looked at in chapter 3, the brothers of the Weston Priory do not actually *do* very much to advance their goals.

I am tempted to say that the Jesuits engage in elite-level politics *universidadamente*, while the Maryknollers engage in mobilization politics evangelistically, and the Benedictines . . . well, the Benedictines engage in a kind of monastic politics through which they pray for a change of heart that would lead themselves and those with whom they interact to embody the values of solidarity and hospitality with which the brothers and sisters try to structure their communal life. But saying that would be too simplistic. The Benedictines—these particular Benedictines anyway—do quite a bit more than pray, and much of what they do is subtly but unmistakably political. In short, these Benedictines work quite hard at responding to the challenges and potential contradictions between Brother Leo's vision of a traditional monastic life of prayer and work, on the one hand, and the Christian responsibilities inherent in citizenship in what they take to be a sinful and suffering world, on the other. This is why the Arco Iris de Alianza is so important to the brothers and sisters, and this is why the Guadalupe Center is the indispensable embodiment of it. The brothers offer their sisters the *mucho respeto* that still lights up the women's eyes, and they extend an invitation to significant participation in a monastic life that is at one and the same time both deeply traditional and appealingly open. And for their part, the sisters offer their brothers an avenue of solidarity and caring: an opportunity for focused engagement with Latin America and its people that the men would never have found on their mountain in rural Vermont.

Together, then, they try to offer an invitation to join them in that transnational combining of the *ora* of the monastery with the *labora* of the mission to bring about a transformation of the heart. One of the brothers told me that he would think it blasphemous if he ever thought of himself as a US citizen over and above thinking of himself as a Benedictine or a Christian. I do not know how many of the people who respond to the brothers' invitation to experience the reality of Latin America in Cuernavaca would admit to such a deep sense of communal and transnational (or even nonnational) identity. But I do know that the brothers and sisters wish to impart to their visitors—both subtly in Vermont, and much less subtly in Mexico—the idea that they all have to take responsibility for the economic and political policies that are propagated in their name, and thereby take responsibility for the people who suffer because of those policies on the southern side of the border.

There are many moments of quiet and hospitality that I will remember of my many visits to the Weston Priory and of my stays at the *casa central* in Mexico City and the Guadalupe Center in Cuernavaca. But perhaps no experience in either place imparted more clearly to me the wider meaning of the Alianza, and the political hope that is embedded within it, than the moment at the Guadalupe Center in Cuernavaca when a gentle, deeply spiritual Mexican sister told the group of visitors from the United States that it was our responsibility to do *something* when we got home about the fact that NAFTA was causing such harm to her—our—brothers and sisters in Mexico. In one sense her words and their jarring political specificity sounded incongruous to me, given the idyllic monastic setting in which she spoke them. On further consideration, however, I realized that her words, and the political challenge to US citizens that they represented, were a major reason that particular setting had come to exist in the first place. The Guadalupe Center, in the City of Eternal Spring, is the concrete manifestation of a transnational religious community that has a clear political dimension. The Rule of Saint Benedict begins by saying that prayer is "the first step in anything worthwhile." But the monks of the Weston Priory and the Misioneras Guadalupanas de Cristo Rey want the many people who come to enjoy their Benedictine hospitality to leave believing that the first step of prayer should be followed by the second step of opening one's heart to a stranger, and to the third, fourth, and fifth steps of taking action to address the poverty and suffering that characterize *la realidad* of Latin America.

CHAPTER 5

Conclusion

R unning through my academic discipline of political science is a powerful assumption that political activities de-
rive the bulk of their meaning from their influence on public policy.
This assumption is not always explicit, and the influence need not
be direct or obvious. But somewhere down the causal chain of activity there ought to be a tangible relationship between the action
being examined and policy. Otherwise, many ask, why examine
it? The first question in summing up and justifying the examinations that have occupied the three central chapters of this book,
therefore, is whether these particular transnational religious communities have had any real influence on US foreign policy towards
Latin America in the circumstances I have detailed. The short answer is that they have. The effects may not always have been direct
and conclusive, but in at least two out of the three transnational
religious communities I have examined—the Jesuit priests and the
Maryknoll missioners—the influence on policy and governmental
action was real and significant. And in the third case—the Benedictine monastics—the participants were not really aiming the bulk
of their efforts at distinct policies or decisions anyway. Instead, in
ways that were wholly consistent with their Benedictine ethos, the
brothers and sisters of the Arco Iris de Alianza were hoping to have
a subtle but tangible effect on American foreign policy by creating
a deeper level of awareness and understanding between the US and
Mexican peoples.

In the first case study, the influence of the Society of Jesus on US
policy in Latin America, or in El Salvador more specifically, can be

summed up in Teresa Whitfield's telling statement: "And then came the Jesuits."[1] As stated in chapter 2, perhaps the greatest mistake the Salvadoran military made in its long and tragic war with the Farabundo Martí National Liberation Front (FMLN) was deciding to silence Ignacio Ellacuría and his Jesuit colleagues by pumping bullets into their heads on the back lawn of the Universidad Centroamericana on November 16, 1989. In fact, that decision was so counterproductive, and frankly so stupid, that it raised a whole host of questions on its own. What was the high command of the Salvadoran military thinking? Did they really expect anyone to fall for their clumsy attempts to pin blame for the murders on the FMLN? After so many years of dealing with Ellacuría and the other Jesuits in El Salvador, did the colonels know nothing about how the Society of Jesus was structured, and did they never even consider how Jesuit priests in the United States—Jesuit college presidents in the United States—would respond to the murder of six of their own in cold blood with weapons paid for by US taxpayers?

The answers to these questions were provided by the murders themselves, of course. The high command apparently really was that clueless, that unsophisticated politically, and so they took the one action that was probably most likely to excite organized opposition in the United States to the policies that supported and funded their murderous schemes. The transnational ties at the heart of the Society of Jesus came to the forefront immediately in the form of Georgetown president Leo O'Donovan's outraged op-ed piece in the *Washington Post* the day after the murders. Those transnational ties then constructed a web of solidarity and support that was perhaps most graphically symbolized by Boston College president Donald Monan's stubborn presence at the mockery of a trial in San Salvador. And the deep commitments and wide networks that defined the "Jesuit family" described by Representative Nancy Pelosi led, in relatively short order after the murders at the UCA, to significant change in US policy towards El Salvador and its military, and to just the kind of negotiated settlement between government and guerilla that the Salvadoran command had been trying to prevent when they killed Ellacuría and the other Jesuits in the first place.

We will return later in this conclusion to the broader implications of these case studies, but it merits mention right away that the Jesuit response to the murder of their own in El Salvador was relatively unique in its specificity and in its efficacy. There were many Jesuits in the United States, of course, who were deeply concerned about El Salvador and about US policies toward that country well before the murders in November 1989. But what really motivated Jesuit priests in the United States to take concerted political action in terms of those policies was the attack on their brothers—the attack, in a sense, on their own religious community by their own government, in the form of its policies regarding El Salvador. And it was the shock of that recognition that led priests and institutional leaders like O'Donovan and Monan to commit their substantial political resources to the task of modifying policies that had implications for El Salvador well beyond a legitimate investigation into the murder of the Jesuit martyrs.

The factors that led Peggy Healy, Nancy Donovan, and their Maryknoll colleagues to take political action in opposition to the contra war in Nicaragua were in some ways quite similar to what motivated the Jesuits. But in other ways the factors that drove the Maryknoll sisters were broader. Like the Jesuit college presidents, the Maryknoll missioners were personally aggrieved and deeply outraged by the murder of two of their own—Ita Ford and Maura Clarke—by basically the same political and military elements within El Salvador who would later kill the Jesuits at the UCA. But for Maryknollers like Healy and Donovan, their transnational connections and their web of solidarity were not so much with Nicaraguan Maryknollers, or even with fellow US citizens working and living in Central America. The Maryknoll sisters were linked in transnational community with all the people of Nicaragua and Central America. The Maryknoll commitment to accompanying these people in their day-to-day struggle to eke out a life of dignity within a context of crushing poverty and seemingly endless war was what led the sisters to a level of political activism both in Central America and back in the United States that none of them could have imagined when they had left their homes years before to work in the missions. As

Nancy Donovan put it: "When I made that decision of getting off that pickup truck and heading off into Contra-controlled territory, I thought a lot of things could happen to me—I could be killed or I could be kidnapped, but I did not think that what would happen would be international fame."[2]

In some ways the sisters' political activism took fairly traditional forms. Nancy Donovan testified before Congress, after all, and Peggy Healy's relationship with Speaker of the House Tip O'Neill was, ironically enough, a classic case of what political scientists call elite or insider lobbying. Nevertheless, the major focus of the sisters' efforts was on an effort to evangelize US citizens by informing them about what was being done in their name and then asking them to speak up in opposition to US policy in Central America. As I will emphasize again in a moment, this commitment to reverse mission on the part of the Maryknollers was entirely consistent with the structures and practices of their own religious community.

To be sure, isolating or detailing the precise political influence of that evangelization is a difficult task. Speaker O'Neill openly admitted that his own growing opposition to Ronald Reagan's policies in Central America was informed and advanced by the information he received from Peggy Healy through her back channel communications from Nicaragua. So to the extent that O'Neill's firm resistance served as the central impediment to President Reagan in implementing support for the contras—whom Reagan called equal to the founding fathers—then the Maryknoll sisters had a significant effect on US policy at that time, or at the very least on the tenor of the debate over that policy between congressional leadership and the White House.[3] But it is also true that any effort to catalogue the exact policy effects of reverse mission in this instance would run into the same conceptual and methodological limitations that bedevil analysis of public opinion on foreign policy in a broader sense. The most that one can say with real confidence in this instance is that the sisters' missionary efforts among middle-class Catholics in the United States probably served more as a brake on policy, in setting the limits of what could not be countenanced, than as a guide on what was done specifically.

Finally, the political dynamics involved in the *alianza* between the monks of the Weston Priory and the Misioneras Guadalupanas de Cristo Rey in Mexico represent a hybrid of the Jesuit and Maryknoll cases. The Benedictine brothers, like the Maryknoll sisters, are obviously motivated to take political action by the friends they have made among the people of Mexico, Nicaragua, and to a lesser extent Brazil. But that concern for the people of Latin America is mediated and animated so clearly and so powerfully through the brothers' relationship with their Benedictine sisters that the political ties between Vermont and Mexico resemble in surprising ways the encircling "ours" that defines and animates the Society of Jesus. One can only imagine the forcefulness of the reaction from Vermont, for example, if an army funded and supported by the US government were ever to cause direct harm to one or more of the Guadalupanas in Mexico.

Short of this unimaginable eventuality, however, the brothers' political activities and their influence on US policy are more akin to the indirect approach that lies at the heart of the Maryknollers' reverse mission. To be sure, the brothers do engage in plenty of direct, policy-based lobbying of their congressional representatives in Vermont. And the brothers did make the politically freighted decision to offer the Ixcot family a secure home on the priory's grounds at the height of the sanctuary movement in 1984. But more than the Jesuits, and in different ways from the Maryknollers, the Benedictines are content to leave many of the details of political activism and policy advocacy to the US citizens who have availed themselves of their hospitality in Weston, Vermont, or especially those who have completed the Faith and Hospitality Experience in Cuernavaca. This is not to imply that the politically meaningful messages that the brothers and sisters convey in the context of that hospitality are subtle, or that the political implications of a greater understanding of *la realidad* are not spelled out for their guests. To the contrary, visitors to the Guadalupe Center are clearly admonished to bring that greater understanding home with them and to use it as a springboard for reforming attitudes in the United States that will, in time, bring about real change in US foreign policy towards Latin America.

Forms of Religious Transnationalism

In the introduction I argued that the political activities being discussed here would be distinctively transnational in nature. Now that I have presented three detailed case studies of three distinctive religious communities, the validity of that original statement seems almost too obvious to emphasize. It seems quite clear that the political activities of these religious bodies (and any influence that they subsequently wield) are based on a foundation of transnational communal identity that motivates and animates participants both within the United States and abroad. Jesuits speak movingly of members of their community, no matter where they might live, as being "ours"; Maryknollers associate themselves profoundly with "the people," regardless of the citizenship that those people hold; and the brothers in Vermont and the sisters in Mexico have infused their Benedictine spirituality and their monastic communities with the cross-border solidarity enshrined in their Arco Iris de Alianza.

Two reasons drew my interest to these transnational religious bonds as a compelling subject of research and analysis. The first is that these kinds of communal bonds and these kinds of political relationships are relatively understudied both in the literature on the making and implementation of US foreign policy and in the literature on the structure of international relations. With the prominent exception of "ethnic lobbying," students of foreign policy tend to give short shrift to the idea that US citizens might develop significant interests in US foreign policies because of the effects that those policies might have on persons and communities with whom those US citizens share powerful bonds of identity and solidarity.

At the same time, students of international relations have, until recently, shown an almost willful disinterest in the role that religion plays in world politics, or in the ways in which religious transnationalism might challenge the state-centric assumptions of the entire field of inquiry. I have chosen to illustrate the limitations of both of these literatures by focusing on the political significance of the transnational links that define Catholic religious orders and congregations in the United States and Latin America. But the basic dynamic sketched out here is relevant to a much wider universe of cases. Margaret Keck and Kathryn Sikkink have written eloquently of the "transnational advocacy networks" that work together to affect practices as diverse as genital mutilation and rain forest depletion.[4] Sidney Tarrow introduced a whole new category of "rooted cosmopolitans" to the discussion of how social movements organize themselves and how those movements seek to influence public policy in a variety of domestic and international settings.[5] If one makes the connection I am trying to draw between these new categories of analysis and the possibilities for policy advocacy within the United States, then it becomes clear that a much more vibrant political process is at work, in terms of the making of US foreign policy, than the old assumptions about a disinterested public might imply.

Certain sectors of the public, it turns out, are decidedly not disinterested in US foreign policy, and that is because those sectors identify themselves and their interests in straightforwardly transnational terms. I have stressed in this book the political vibrancy of transnational *religious* identity, and others have done so in terms of ethnicity. But similar dynamics are also at work in terms of demography, ideology, and even in terms of what Peter Haas has called epistemology.[6] Feminists in the United States, for example, can be mobilized to advance the interests of women who are oppressed by nations with which the United States has close and supportive relations. American environmentalists can try to ease the tasks of their fellow activists abroad by pressuring the US government to get foreign governments to change policies and practices that cause environmental degradation across the globe. And scientists from the United States and around the world can band together as "epistemic communities" to work in solidarity together, as scientists, to address global problems like nuclear proliferation, communicable disease, or, perhaps most prominently in our own day, climate change.

Similarly, it may also be possible for members of other transnational communities to manifest the same kind of double-rootedness that so clearly characterizes the life experiences of these religious orders and congregations. What we have seen with Jesuit priests, Maryknoll missioners, and Benedictine monastics is that their ties to the religious communities to which they belong can come to rival, if not supersede, the national identities that define their citizenship.

Nancy Donovan, for example, was not really a cosmopolitan in the sense that Tarrow might have meant the term. It was not that she had reached out from her home community to participate in a confederation of like-minded activists from other countries. Instead, she left behind her family and home and rooted herself deeply in the Maryknoll Congregation and in their accompaniment of the suffering people of Nicaragua. For the monks in Weston, their sense of belonging to their Benedictine community was, if possible, even stronger and more deeply foundational than the connections that bound the Maryknoller missioners to those whom they called "the people." Living a lifetime in rural isolation with a small group of other monks, these men were able to come fairly close to rejecting their national identities in favor of an intense communal identity that they shared with each other and, portentously, with the Benedictine sisters in Mexico. In neither case, however, did the Maryknoll missioners or the Benedictine monks ever really sever their roots in the United States. And it was those roots after all—those privileges and possibilities of US citizenship—that proved so politically useful in terms of advancing the religious community's interests within the US policymaking processes. These professed, lifelong members of transnational religious communities really did have both feet rooted in both places, if such a metaphorical contortion is physically possible. To use a loaded phrase from a more parochial past: These Catholic men and women lived lives of dual loyalty that were dynamic, catalytic, and (perhaps) harbingers of a transnational phenomenon that will become only more common in our increasingly globalized world.

Founding and Mission

The conclusion that has emerged most clearly from this examination of the Society of Jesus, the Maryknoll Congregation, and the Benedictine Confederation, however, is that all of these transnational ties and all of this political influence are utterly dependent on the particular institutional structures and communal missions that characterize these various transnational religious bodies in the first place. As I suggest at the very start of this book, political action in any given context grows out of the nature of the transnationalism itself, both in terms of structural linkages and, in the case of the religious ties I have examined, in terms of the religious mission, or what the participants in these relationships would probably call the founding charism of their order or community. I cannot see any reason why similar dynamics would not also be true in terms of nonreligious transnational communities as well. Nonreligious communities might have less clearly defined founding principles and perhaps less obviously particularistic institutional structures than do organizations like the Society of Jesus or the Maryknoll Congregation or the Benedictine Confederation. But all transnational links are built upon some form of founding motivation, purpose, or mission, and all are also experienced and mediated through structural modalities of one form or another. One of the implications of the arguments I have made concerning religious communities and Catholic religious orders is that the political activism of all transnational communities will be shaped, driven, and given political meaning by these factors of structure and mission.

I do not want to overstate the significance of a founding tradition, but it is nevertheless obvious that the Society of Jesus continues to exhibit the military structure and at least outward disciplinary ethos instituted by its founder, Saint Ignatius of Loyola, nearly half a millennium ago. This community of men (I will return to this distinction shortly), with its highly structured Spiritual Exercises and its palpable esprit de corps, is at its center a relatively insular band of brothers that defines itself with the collective formulation of "ours." Like marines who would never countenance leaving a fallen comrade on the field of battle, the Jesuits in the United States of America were shocked into recognition and action by the murder of their six brothers at the Universidad Centroamericana in San Salvador in November 1989. And consistent with their spirit of identification with each other, Jesuits in both El Salvador and the United States mobilized their considerable personal and institutional resources to demand changes in the US policies that could allow such monstrous events to take place, and to demand that commitments be made in Washington and in El Salvador to pursue a more aggressive investigation of the murders themselves.

The contrast between the Jesuit fathers living in the United States and the Maryknoll sisters living in Nicaragua should not be overdrawn, but it also should not be ignored. For the women of Maryknoll, successors after all to the Maryknoll secretaries of the early twentieth century, the founding spirit of their community is one of service and accompaniment of "the people" through the trials and tribulations of their daily lives. Of course, Maryknoll sisters were outraged when two of their own were murdered in El Salvador, and in many ways that murder was as foundational for the sisters as the deaths at the UCA were for the Jesuits. As Peggy Healy put it, the murders in 1980 "profoundly changed everyone."[7] But it is also true that women like Nancy Donovan and Peggy Healy were working at a different level of transnational identification than men like Leo O'Donovan and Joseph O'Hare were. The Maryknollers were members of a very different kind of transnational community than the Jesuits were. The sisters were missionaries; and given their evolving understanding of that specific vocation, "the people" was a refrain that dominated everything that the Maryknollers thought and said about their work in Central America. Identification with the sufferings of those people was what motivated Donovan to testify before Congress, Healy to cajole Tip O'Neill, and so many of their sisters to travel around the United States to publicize the harm that their government was doing to their people in Nicaragua. In short, when the interests of "the people" were threatened and harmed by US foreign policy, these Maryknoll sisters did what their foundress had called them to do decades before. They evangelized; they went out to the missions, in this case places like Connecticut and Michigan and California, and they tried "to spread the Good News of the Reign of God."[8]

This matter of political activism being consistent with institutional structure and founding missions might be even more clearly evident in the case of the Benedictines. The transnational ties between the monks in Vermont and the Guadalupanas in Mexico, and the activities that grow out of those ties, are based openly, deeply, and portentously in the Benedictine principle of hospitality. Everything these two communities do together can best be understood in terms of that principle. From the designation of the monastery in Vermont as a sanctuary for the Ixcots, to the establishment of the Guadalupe Center for the purpose of introducing *la realidad* of Latin America to visitors from *el Norte*, all is distinctly Benedictine in structure and ethos. The brothers of the Weston Priory are monks—cenobites in Benedict's parlance—while the Guadalupanas are themselves missionaries, in many ways quite similar to the Maryknoll sisters. The difference between the monastic commitment in Vermont and the missionary activity in Mexico indicates the wide diversity of approach that is possible within the Benedictine tradition. But the close and persistent ties codified in the Alianza also show how deeply ingrained hospitality is in the Benedictine tradition itself. While Jesuit fathers cohere around "ours," and Maryknoll sisters devote themselves to accompanying "the people," the brothers in Vermont and the sisters in Mexico have dedicated themselves to accompanying each other.

I do not mean this observation to denigrate in any way the devotion that the Misioneras Guadalupanas demonstrate to the people they live among and administer to throughout Mexico and the rest of Latin America. But I do mean to emphasize that the Alianza itself is almost paradigmatically Benedictine in its conception and in its implementation. The brothers offer the sisters the quiet of Brother Leo's monastery and an organic connection to the traditional practices of the Benedictine monastic traditions. In return, the sisters offer the brothers a pathway to pastoral service and to an ongoing interaction with people outside of their monastic walls that has become a central aspect of the monks' own communal life. And in what can only be described as a powerful symbol of their Confederation's charism, the whole thing is based and grounded in a house, a residence in Cuernavaca, Mexico. That house is a shared home for the sisters and their brothers, of course. But it is also designed to welcome visitors from the United States and to thereby effect a spiritual and political awakening across the United States–Mexico border through the provision of Benedictine hospitality.

Fathers, Brothers, and Sisters

The significance of varied institutional modalities might well go beyond the very different forms of transnational structure and mission that characterize these three communities. As I say in chapter 1, these three transnational communities also differ from each other along what we might call demographic axes. What is the significance in terms of forms of political action, for example, of the fact that the Jesuits I examined are all men, the Maryknollers I examined are all women, but the Benedictines studied here are a mixture of the two? I will not be the first analyst to begin such a discussion by admitting that it is difficult to specify in concrete terms the influence of sex difference on behavior of any kind, nor will I be the first to caution that such differences should be treated gingerly, with a clear acknowledgment that sex ought not to be considered facilely determinative. Yet, with all of that said and duly noted, one cannot help but point out, for example, that the transnational linkages that powerfully define the Society of Jesus are shaped by the fact that all of the participants in that particular transnational community are male.

When I termed the Jesuits a "band of brothers" earlier, I did so advisedly, just as I did when I used a military analogy to describe how the designation of "ours" actually articulates itself in practice. The use of the term "fraternity" might be judged by some as an insult, and I certainly do not wish to offend. But there is, nevertheless, something of a distinctively fraternal solidarity implied in an all-male "society" that has never, as many other Catholic orders have, opened its doors to women, nor even associated itself closely with female communities of one kind or another. To be a Jesuit is to be, by definition, a male, something that is not true of the designation Maryknoller or Benedictine. Moreover, to be a Jesuit college president in the 1980s was to hold a traditionally male position (less so in the intervening years) and to have access to traditionally male instruments of political influence, such as institutional resources and high-level political connections. To be sure, it is not all that hard to imagine leaders of a female community mustering their institutional resources in the same way that Leo O'Donovan or Joseph

O'Hare did in the fall of 1989 in response to the murders at the UCA. But, of course, O'Donovan, as president of Georgetown, and O'Hare, as president of Fordham, were holding positions at that time that were only open to men, and their instinctive decision to apply the resources of their positions to very traditional forms of political advocacy were perfectly in keeping with the traditional all-male structures of their religious community.

"Maryknoll," on the other hand, is a designation that can be applied to men or women. Indeed, the original Catholic Missionary Society of America, as indicated earlier, was restricted to men, and it was only some years later that Mollie Rogers (later Mary Joseph Rogers) was able to found the separate but closely affiliated Foreign Mission Sisters of Saint Dominic. Their original designation as "the secretaries" is long since dead, and there is nothing at all submissive about the work and commitment of the women I have described here as they live their lives and carry out their mission in Central America and elsewhere. Nevertheless, I detected a strong ethos of humble service among the many Maryknoll women I talked with while conducting this research. And I also heard strong echoes of the particular sensitivity to the needs of women that characterized the original Maryknoll sisters who carried out the Kaying experiment in China more than fifty years ago. To be sure, many men in many contexts devote themselves to "accompanying the people" in their lives of daily struggle. But with all the passage of time, and despite all the changes in sex roles that have taken place, I came away from my examinations of these communities with the impression that the Maryknoll women, more than a half century later, still find it somewhat easier (if that is the right word) than men do to go out two by two, or five by five, or ten by ten, to find the poor and move in next door to them.[9]

An important part of that difference, I think, is inherent in the specifically Catholic reality that these women are, by definition, not ordained priests. This is not the place for a detailed examination of the history of clericalism in the Catholic Church. But in a traditionally patriarchal setting such as Latin America, the designation of "father" has a distancing effect that the title "sister" does not create in a similar way. In fact, the very words "father" and "sister" speak volumes about the differing social and pastoral roles that the two designations imply. And I would argue that those social and pastoral roles in turn affect the kinds of political mobilization and policy advocacy that the two communities, Jesuits and Maryknollers, pursue—in Latin America, in the United States, and, most importantly, transnationally. Obviously, these roles are not ironclad; and just as obviously, we can identify cases where members of each community have adopted the approach most characteristic of the other. Peggy Healy, for example, was deeply involved in very traditional political activities in Washington in the mid-1980s, although one can probably safely assume that she was the only woman in the room when she was meeting with Speaker O'Neill and his top aides. But the pervasive identification with the people, and the evangelizing devotion to reverse mission as a political strategy, are more in keeping with the ethos of a community of nonordained women than with that of a society of male priests.

We have seen these dynamics of clerical status and sex identity most clearly in the case of the Arco Iris de Alianza between Vermont and Mexico. As described in chapter 4, the two Benedictine communities exhibit an uninhibited devotion to each other that, although wholly chaste, is clearly grounded in the unavoidable fact that the brothers are men and the sisters are women. The passionate caring that members express and manifest for each other is palpable, compelling, and frankly impossible to imagine between two communities of men or two communities of women. At the same time, the very name that the brothers and sisters have given to their covenant denotes their own recognition of the special nature of their ties to each other. The rainbow symbolism invoked in the term *arco iris* was explicitly meant as a reference to the span tying the two communities together as men and women, as well as to the geographic distance between them as residents of the United States and Mexico.

To use a familial analogy, the Jesuits are brothers to each other, but the Benedictines are brothers and sisters to each other, and that appears to make a real difference in how they interact and how they support each other. At the risk of invoking stereotypes, I think that anyone who has experienced sibling relationships within their own family can attest to the different textures that generally define these relationships. For lack of a better word, I would say that the transnational solidarity that gave birth to the Guadalupe Center in Cuernavaca is defined by a *tenderness* between the brothers and sisters that infuses all of their cross-border interactions, a tenderness that deeply influences the depth in which the brothers identify with the pastoral mission that their sisters are pursuing in Mexico.

This quality should not come as a surprise if we recall that the sisters' initial reaction to the brothers' overture of friendship was an enthusiastic celebration and embrace of the fact that they were being treated with such respect *by men*. Used to the assumption of their nonclerical, subservient position in a patriarchal church, both local and universal, the Guadalupanas recognized in the monks from Weston a group of men—Benedictine men—with whom they as women—Benedictine women—could develop a relationship of equality, respect, and mutual support. "We no longer had fathers," they said. "We had brothers."[10] And this recognition, of course, was a direct function of Abbott Leo's revolutionary commitment to eradicating clericalism and hierarchy at the Weston Priory by erasing the traditional barriers between choir monks and lay brothers.

I have spent a considerable amount of time in recent years at the priory, and I can personally attest to the lack of these barriers among the brothers today. To be sure, the monks need at least some ordained priests within their community to perform the Catholic sacraments that are at the heart of the priory's devotional practices. But none of the brothers is ever addressed as "father." No distinction is maintained in the community's day-to-day life between the ordained and the lay, and I would not even have known who the ordained members were if not for the fact that I have observed mass at the priory on a number of occasions. It is this small but crucial denial of hierarchical status and distinction, I am convinced, that allowed the brothers to be so readily accepted by the sisters in the first place, and it is this foundational commitment to egalitarianism that remains such a critical element in the respect and mutuality that continues to animate the Alianza more than thirty years after its establishment. These ties between Vermont and Mexico are unique, in my experience, and they set the stage for a form of transnational solidarity—and a method of political mobilization—that is familial, enduring, and remarkably intimate.

Not all transnational relationships, religious or otherwise, will exhibit this level of closeness or identification. Sometimes the ties may be as close as, or closer than, those that characterize a family separated by migration or exile, or a national population scattered in a global diaspora. Sometimes transnational community might involve adopted identities and affective solidarity with peoples from other lands. And sometimes these relationships will be more organizational, corporate if you will, and based on shared membership in international societies of one sort or another. In all cases, however, the political actions that arise out of these transnational connections will be powerfully shaped by the factors identified in this concluding chapter: the structural nature of the transnational community itself; the mission or purpose that the community has devoted itself to, particularly in its formative stage; and finally the nature of the membership of the community, particularly in terms of demographic or institutional categorizations that might affect levels of interaction and forms of communication.

My intention in *Reverse Mission* has been to show, through attention to three particular forms of transnational religious community, that these kinds of political relationships are vibrant, meaningful, and ever more prominent in an international arena in which state borders are increasingly blurred, and in which global civil society is more and more robust. More specifically, my intention has been to demonstrate that transnational relationships—and the political mobilizations that arise out of them—can play significant roles in the making of US foreign policy, and by extension the making of the foreign policies of other state actors in world politics. US citizens, in other words, can be powerfully motivated by the experiences of their brothers and sisters in other countries, particularly when those experiences are negatively affected through actions taken by the US government in Washington, DC. In such cases—in cases like those I have detailed in this book—US citizens will engage in various forms of reverse mission to use their own levers of political power for the purposes of offering support to community members who would never have access to American politics in any other way. As Nancy

Donovan put it so clearly, when one's own government is doing harm to one's own people, then the political imperative to try to do something about it is obvious and undeniable. Indeed, as one of the monks at the Weston concluded so graphically: To ignore that imperative, and to think of oneself in merely national terms, would be for a member of a transnational religious community nothing less than blasphemous.

Notes

Chapter 1

1. See Laswell, *Politics*.

2. A recently published review of the literature on the relationship between religious affiliation and voting referred to the "ethnoreligious perspective" from which political actions are taken on the basis of "the centrality of religious belonging." See Smidt, Kellstedt, and Guth, "Role of Religion," 5.

3. This dominant mode of classification was reflected most clearly, and most famously, in Herberg, *Protestant, Catholic, Jew*.

4. The literature on this matter is, of course, extensive. For a good introduction see Wilcox and Larson, *Onward Christian Soldiers*.

5. Such religious solidarity can at times be mobilized on a relatively massive scale, such as in the case of the concerns expressed by evangelical Christians about treatment of their coreligionists abroad. See Hertzke, *Freeing God's Children*.

6. The latest prominent installment in this controversy is represented by Mearsheimer and Walt, *Israel Lobby*.

7. A particularly blunt expression of this sentiment occurred on television when Glenn Beck said to Keith Ellison, the first Muslim ever elected to the US Congress: "Sir, prove to me that you are not working with our enemies." *CNN Headline News*, November 14, 2006.

8. This charge of course was most famously leveled in Blanshard, *American Freedom and Catholic Power*.

9. Most famously, vice presidential candidate Geraldine Ferraro was sharply challenged in 1984 over her position on abortion by her own archbishop in New York. See Byrnes, *Catholic Bishops in American Politics*, 108–26.

10. Ryall, "Church as a Transnational Actor," 47.

11. In fact, I have published such a book myself. See Byrnes, *Transnational Catholicism*. But also see Rudolph and Piscatori, *Transnational Religion and Fading States*.

12. Berger, *De-secularization of the World*.

13. The classic expression of this viewpoint is found in Waltz, *Theory of International Politics*.

14. A helpful introduction to this school of thought is Katzenstein, *Between Power and Plenty*.

15. Truman, *Governmental Process*.

16. Glazer and Moynihan, *Ethnicity*, 24.

17. Mathias, "Ethnic Groups," 981.

18. For two prominent and representative contributions to this debate, see Shain, "Multicultural Foreign Policy," and Huntington, "The Erosion of American National Interests."

19. Hertzke, *Representing God in Washington*, 114.

20. See Ahrari, *Ethnic Groups*, especially 155–58.

21. Ibid., 156.

22. Ibid.

23. Mearsheimer and Walt, *Israel Lobby*, especially 49–77.

24. Ahrari, *Ethnic Groups*, 156 (emphasis in original).

25. I can cite my own family as an example in this regard. Almost all of my ancestors came to the United States from Ireland, and my extended family maintains a vague sense of Irish cultural identity. But despite attending parades on Saint Patrick's Day or giving our children Irish names, I do not detect among my siblings or cousins any politically meaningful attachment to the plight of the Irish in Ireland. In any event, almost all of those children, because of ethnic intermarriage, are only half Irish American anyway.

26. See Walsh, *Sin and Censorship*.

27. There was a time in the early 1980s when Catholic opinion was influenced by the bishops' opposition to US defense policy in regard to nuclear weapons. But other than that specific period of time and an occasional expression of concern for the rights of Catholics in China or some other place where those rights are seen to be imperiled, Catholic interests among the vast American laity are not generally organized and expressed along these lines.

28. Ahrari, *Ethnic Groups*, 157.

29. Actually, a couple of the monks at the Weston Priory are not themselves native-born US citizens, a significant fact to which I return in chapter 4.

30. Keohane and Nye, *Transnational Relations*, xii. For two examples of voluminous literature, see Walzer, *Toward a Global Civil Society*, and Batliwala and Brown, *Transnational Civil Society*.

31. Keck and Sikkink, *Activists beyond Borders*, 12.

32. Ibid.

33. Tarrow, *New Transnational Activism*, 29.

34. Ibid., 29, 2.

35. Ibid., 3.

36. Ibid., 29.

37. I am grateful to Sidney Tarrow himself for pointing out to me the possibility that the members of these particular religious communities might be doubly rooted politically.

38. Risse-Kappen, "Bringing Transnational Relations Back In."

39. Rudolph and Piscatori, *Transnational Religion and Fading States*.

NOTES TO PAGES 29–39   171

Chapter 2

1. The best "chronology of the crime" is given in the chapter by that name in Doggett, *Death Foretold*, 37–71.

2. This phrase, "service of faith and the promotion of justice," appears frequently in chapter 4 of the documents of the Thirty-Second General Congregation of the Jesuits and has become over the ensuing years an accepted shorthand among Jesuits for the definition of their community's mission.

3. Beirne, "Ordinary People Made Extraordinary"; and Charles Beirne, interview with the author, Syracuse, NY.

4. Beirne, "Ordinary People Made Extraordinary."

5. Brackley, "El Salvador"; and Dean Brackley, interview with the author, San Salvador.

6. Brackley, "El Salvador."

7. For an extensive account of the lives of the murdered priests, with a particular emphasis on Ellacuría, see Whitfield, *Paying the Price*.

8. For instructive biographical material on Ignatius Loyola and on his founding of the Society of Jesus, see Ganss, *Ignatius Loyola*, especially 10–48.

9. Robert Mitchell, interview with the author, New York, NY.

10. Beirne, interview with the author, Syracuse, NY.

11. Brackley, "El Salvador."

12. The Spiritual Exercises are reprinted in Ganss, *Ignatius Loyola*, 113–214.

13. Beirne, interview with the author, Syracuse, NY.

14. Brackley, interview with the author, San Salvador.

15. Paul Locatelli, interview with the author, Santa Clara, CA.

16. Leo O'Donovan, interview with the author, Washington, DC.

17. Donald Monan, interview with the author, Boston, MA.

18. Pat Burns, correspondence with the author, March 11, 2005. Burns was president of the Jesuit Conference at the time of the murders.

19. O'Donovan, interview with the author, Washington, DC.

20. O'Donovan, "Martyrdom and Mercy."

21. O'Donovan, interview with the author, Washington, DC.

22. Joseph O'Hare, interview with the author, New York, NY.

23. The homily was reprinted in *America*, December 16, 1989. See O'Hare, "In Solidarity."

24. Extensive information on the AJCU and its activities is available at www.ajcunet.edu.

25. Monan, interview with the author, Boston, MA.

26. The same point was made by José María Tojeira in an interview with the author, San Salvador. Tojeira was the Jesuit provincial in Central America at the time of the murders. He is now the rector of the UCA.

27. The telling phrase "intellectual authors" was coined by Tojeira and was used throughout the period as a way of placing pressure on the Salvadoran government to investigate the murders more aggressively. Tojeira, interview with the author, San Salvador.

28. O'Hare, interview with the author, New York, NY.

29. Monan, interview with the author, Boston, MA.

30. Grande's murder is placed in the broader context of religion's place in Latin America in Lernoux, *Cry of the People*, 67–75.

31. Whitfield, *Paying the Price*, 104.

32. Lernoux, *Cry of the People*, 76.

33. For an extended account of Romero's so-called conversion see Sobrino, *Witnesses to the Kingdom*, 15–28. Jon Sobrino was the only member of the on-campus Jesuit community at the UCA who was not killed on November 16, 1989. He happened to be at a speaking engagement in Thailand at the time.

34. Ibid., 18.

35. See, in particular, Romero, *Voice of the Voiceless*.

36. Romero, quoted in Brockman, *Romero*, 255.

37. Romero, quoted in ibid., 242.

38. Sobrino, *Witnesses to the Kingdom*, 13.

39. Ellacuría, quoted in ibid., 53.

40. The term *universidadamente* is from Beirne, "Ordinary People Made Extraordinary."

41. Whitfield, *Paying the Price*, 38 (emphasis in original).

42. Arrupe, quoted in ibid., 38.

43. *Documents of the 31st and 32nd General Congregations*, 421, 427–28.

44. Ibid., 426–27.

45. All of the following quotes are from Ellacuría's commencement address.

46. Cerna's testimony and the controversy surrounding it are covered in Doggett, *Death Foretold*, 218–21, and Whitfield, *Paying the Price*, 73–90. The account here, unless otherwise cited, is based on those two sources.

47. "Witness Links Killers," *New York Times*, November 28, 1989.

48. "Dispute in Salvador," *New York Times*, December 11, 1989.

49. Tojeira, interview with the author, San Salvador.

50. "Witnesses in Jesuit Slayings," *New York Times*, December 18, 1989.

51. Beirne, interview with the author, Syracuse, NY.

52. Francisco Estrada, interview with the author, San Salvador.

53. This account of efforts to relieve the UCA's debt is based mostly on the recollections of Beirne, interview with the author, Syracuse, NY.

54. O'Hare, interview with the author, New York.

55. See in particular on this point, Doggett, *Death Foretold*, and Whitfield, *Paying the Price*.

56. 135 Cong. Rec. 30,430 (1989).

57. Whitfield, *Paying the Price*, 83.

58. Luis Calero, interview with the author, Santa Clara, CA.

59. O'Donovan, interview with the author, Washington, DC.

60. Locatelli, interview with the author, Santa Clara, CA.

61. 135 Cong. Rec. 31,763 (1989).

62. 135 Cong. Rec. 30,419 (1989).

63. 135 Cong. Rec. 30,097 (1989).

64. 135 Cong. Rec. 30,432 (1989).

65. Ahrari, *Ethnic Groups*, 156.

66. Joseph Moakley, quoted in "Slain Jesuits Endure," *Boston Globe*, November 16, 1990.

67. Whitfield, *Paying the Price*, 83.

68. The indispensable treatment of the investigation and trial is in Doggett, *Death Foretold*.

69. "Salvador Leader Links," *New York Times*, January 8, 1990.

70. The UCA was in a sector of the city that was firmly controlled by the military in mid-November, not by the FMLN. All but the most obviously self-interested observers noted from the beginning that it would have been impossible for guerillas to have even pierced the government-controlled sector to gain access to the UCA, much less to have spent over two hours on the campus shouting orders, killing the priests, shooting off flares to signal the completion of the operation, and even drinking some beer before heading back out into the city.

71. Again the definitive source on these matters is Doggett, *Death Foretold*.

72. Ibid., 109–20.

73. Moakley, quoted in "Justice Disserved," *Washington Post*, October 14, 1991.

74. Monan, interview with the author, Boston, MA.

75. Beirne, interview with the author, Syracuse, NY.

76. Commission on the Truth for El Salvador, *From Madness to Hope*.

77. Those complexities are given full treatment in Montgomery, *Revolution in El Salvador*, 213–61.

78. Whitfield, *Paying the Price*, 374.

79. Ibid., 380.

80. Roberto Pineda Guerra, quoted in ibid., 74.

81. Richard Buhler, quoted in "Slain Jesuits Endure," *Boston Globe*.

82. Buhler, quoted in ibid.

83. Steven Privett, interview with the author, San Francisco, CA.

Chapter 3

1. *Hearing before the Subcommittee on Western Hemisphere Affairs of the Committee on Foreign Affairs, House of Representatives,* 99th Cong. 268–69 (April 16, 17, 18, 1985).

2. In a speech to a conservative political group in 1985, Reagan said that the Nicaraguan contras were "our brothers," "freedom fighters," and "the moral equal of our Founding Fathers, and the brave men and women of the French Resistance." Quoted in Boyd, "Reagan Terms Nicaraguan Rebels."

3. Nancy Donovan, quoted in Everett, *Bearing Witness, Building Bridges,* 145.

4. The phrase appears in Maryknoll Sisters of Saint Dominic, *Complementary Document,* 4. This prosaic definition is given to "reverse mission": "We participate in mission education and fund raising among the people in our home countries during periods of renewal and/or when giving Congregational Service at the Center."

5. Donovan, interview with the author, Ossining, NY.

6. Ibid.

7. Maryknoll Sisters of Saint Dominic, *Constitutions,* 5, 7, 10.

8. The name was formally changed in 1954 to the Maryknoll Sisters of Saint Dominic. See ibid., ix–x.

9. Robert, *American Women in Mission,* 322.

10. Nevins, *Adventures of Men of Maryknoll.*

11. Lernoux, *Hearts on Fire,* xxxi.

12. Ibid., 66, 62.

13. Mollie Rogers, quoted in Robert, *American Women in Mission,* 349.

14. Cogan, *Sisters of Maryknoll,* especially 26–38.

15. As an example, see Sister Maria del Rey, *Her Name Is Mercy.*

16. Neal, *From Nuns to Sisters.*

17. Second Vatican Council, *Pastoral Constitution,* sec. 4.

18. Robert, *American Women in Mission,* 392.

19. Lernoux, *Hearts on Fire,* 6.

20. Roper, quoted in ibid., 248.

21. Kita, *What Prize Awaits Us,* 8, 40.

22. Ford, *Here I Am Lord,* 100.

23. Maryknoll Sisters of Saint Dominic, *Constitutions,* ix.

24. Terry Alexander, interview with the author, San Salvador.

25. Quoted in Lernoux, *Hearts on Fire,* 143.

26. Peggy Healy, interview with the author, New York, NY.

27. Ibid.

28. See Lernoux, *Hearts on Fire,* 16. For a sense of how events were viewed at the time, see also Donovan, *Pagoda and the Cross.*

29. Lernoux, *Hearts on Fire*, 16.

30. Dohen, *Nationalism and American Catholicism.*

31. Blanshard, *American Freedom and Catholic Power.*

32. Francis Spellman, quoted in Dohen, *Nationalism and American Catholicism*, 1.

33. Sister Mary Victoria, *Nun in Red China.*

34. Cogan, *Sisters of Maryknoll*, 40.

35. See Lernoux, *Hearts on Fire*, 138.

36. The events are described in Noone, *Same Fate*, 56–57.

37. Healy, interview with the author, New York, NY.

38. Ibid.

39. Noone, *Same Fate.*

40. The searing ramifications of this quote are highlighted in Dullea, "Memories of Death Linger."

41. This claim aroused particularly sharp outrage at the time. As an example, see Lewis, "Showing His Colors."

42. Healy, interview with the author, New York, NY.

43. Lernoux, *Hearts on Fire*, 244.

44. Healy, interview with the author, New York, NY.

45. Noone, *Same Fate*, 75, 77–78.

46. Berrigan, *The Trial of the Catonsville Nine.*

47. Melville and Melville, *Guatemala*, 291.

48. Ibid., 296.

49. Lernoux, *Hearts on Fire*, 222. For a broader context from McLaughlin's own point of view, see also McLaughlin, *On the Frontline.*

50. Healy, interview with the author, New York, NY.

51. Ibid.

52. Ibid.

53. Ibid.

54. Hertzke, *Representing God in Washington*, 78.

55. Healy, interview with the author, New York, NY.

56. Ibid.

57. Tip O'Neill, quoted in Taubman, "Speaker and His Sources."

58. O'Neill, quoted in Jimmy Breslin, "Nicaragua, Lady Liberty, and Crack."

59. See Farrell, *Tip O'Neill*, 612–13.

60. Reagan, quoted in Boyd, "Reagan Terms Nicaraguan Rebels."

61. Letter from Healy to O'Neill, quoted in Taubman, "Speaker and His Sources."

62. O'Neill, quoted in Taubman, "Speaker and His Sources." The indirect influence went well beyond Speaker O'Neill, of course. Tom Downey, a Democratic representative from Long Island, NY, suggested that the talks

Maryknoll sisters had given in his district had an "astonishing impact." When visiting constituents insisted that he discuss Central America with them, and he in turn asked them where they had heard about it, they would respond, "Well, this nun came to talk." See Seib, "Catholic and Other Church Groups Oppose."

63. Yehle, "Sister with Spunk."

64. Donovan, quoted in Hillyer, "Missionary Recalls Capture."

65. Donovan, quoted in DeChillo, "Maryknoll Pursues Its Vision."

66. Donovan, quoted in Donziger, "Kidnapped American Nun Blames U.S. Government."

67. Donovan, quoted in Abrams, "Kidnapped Nun Gives Eyewitness Account."

68. Donovan, quoted in Winter, "Faith in the War Zone."

69. Donovan, quoted in Laskiewicz, "Nun Contends U.S. Errs."

70. Donovan, quoted in Leukhardt, "Speakers Rap U.S. Aid."

71. Donovan, quoted in Nathanson, "American Nun Recounts Violence."

72. Donovan, quoted in Fraze, "Tales of Nicaraguan Torture."

73. Donovan, quoted in Ewald, "Maryknoll Recounts Her Kidnapping."

74. Donovan, quoted in Laskiewicz, "Nun Contends U.S. Errs."

75. Donovan, quoted in Hillyer, "Missionary Recalls Capture."

76. Donovan, quoted in Healion, "Nun Disagrees with Reagan."

77. Donovan, quoted in Pattee, "Nun Brings a Message."

78. William Buckley, quoted in DeChillo, "Maryknoll Pursues Its Vision."

79. Michael Novak, quoted in Ostling, "Those Beleaguered Maryknollers."

80. Healy, interview with the author, New York, NY.

81. Maryknoll Sisters of Saint Dominic, Constitutions, 5.

Chapter 4

1. Arco Iris de Alianza is best translated as Rainbow Alliance, a metaphoric reference to the brothers and sisters' belief that their relationship, like a rainbow, spans the usual divides between the United States and Mexico and between Benedictine communities of men and women.

2. The quotes are from the brothers of the Weston Priory, interviews with the author, Weston, VT. I have decided not to identify the names of individual members of these two Benedictine communities either in the text or in notes citing direct quotes. That decision allows me to respect the confidentiality of individual members of what are in many ways quite private communities. More importantly, however, citing statements as having come

from either the brothers or sisters as a whole is in my judgment a more accurate reflection of the remarkably communal atmospheres I encountered
when I visited and spoke with the two communities.

3. Benedict, *Saint Benedict's Rule*, 45 (prologue, para. 1). All references
in this chapter to the *Rule* are taken from this source.

4. Ibid., 51 (chap. 1, para. 1).

5. Ibid., 60 (chap. 4, para. 3); 60 (chap. 4, para. 5); 89 (chap. 22, para. 2);
81 (chap. 16, para. 1); 74 (chap. 8, para. 1).

6. Ibid., 110 (chap. 42, para. 1); 117 (chap. 48, para. 1); 123 (chap. 53,
para. 1).

7. Rembert Weakland, interview with the author, Milwaukee, WI.

8. Hammond, *Benedictine Legacy of Peace*, 215. This volume is an indispensable history of the Weston Priory, written by one of the brothers. Also
helpful in providing background material on the monks is a documentary
film titled *With One Heart*, by David Skillicorn.

9. It was then therefore a "claustral priory," in Benedictine nomenclature. See Hammond, *Benedictine Legacy of Peace*, 314.

10. The story of the founding can be found in ibid., especially 72–92.

11. Ibid., 140, 89. Leo Rudloff said of Weston later in his life that there
he "found a true monastic life . . . a life of devotion, centered in community,
with an intensity which I never found . . . elsewhere—a life that does not
gravitate towards all kinds of activities, but rather towards the *center*, a life of
intense living and growing together, and thus towards God in Christ" (ibid.,
269, emphasis in original).

12. Hammond addresses these issues throughout his book, *Benedictine
Legacy of Peace*, but they are addressed most directly in 92–97 and 136–38.

13. Ibid., 277.

14. Ibid., 276–80.

15. Ibid., 296–97.

16. Hammond describes the dynamic this way: "The Weston Monks realized that the liturgical music they were creating for their own prayer spoke
not only to the prayer-needs of other religious communities far and wide,
but to the broader spectrum of social issues. The Priory's new higher profile
brought invitations and pleas for involvement in movements for disarma-
ment, peace, justice, and social change." Ibid., 270.

17. Ibid., 258.

18. It is interesting to note that Hammond attributed some of this interest on the part of the priory to events that I discussed in earlier chapters. His
sense of chronology is a bit off, but his words are nevertheless instructive,
in terms of the brothers' views as well as their motivations: "Following the
deaths of four North American women missionaries in El Salvador [which
happened four years *after* the brothers first visited the sisters in Mexico], the

community's voice was raised in public confrontation with the United States government over its complicity in the carnage wreaked by U.S.-trained military officers from that region. As this awareness widened, the brothers sought a closer relationship with the people of Latin America." Ibid., 271.

19. This quote is from an unpublished history of the community, a copy of which was given to me by the sisters in Mexico City. "Una nueva vida religiosa," 54.

20. The following section is based mostly on the sisters' self-published communal history, "Una nueva vida religiosa." I received indispensable aid in translating and reading this document from Javier Padilla.

21. I discussed this notion of a "rooted cosmopolitan" at some length in the introduction of this book. The phrase was coined in Tarrow, *New Transnational Activism*.

22. Maryknoll Sisters of Saint Dominic, *Constitutions*, 5.

23. For a wide-ranging discussion of the foundational role that *la Virgen* has played in Mexican national identity, see Brading, *Mexican Phoenix*.

24. This fascinating and freighted period in Mexican history is recounted in Meyer, *Cristero Rebellion*.

25. This quotation is from the 2006 DVD *Guadalupe Center* that was produced by the two communities as a chronicle of their relationship. I am grateful to Rebekah Saylors of Lees McRae College for helping me procure a copy of the DVD while we were in Cuernavaca together.

26. Misioneras Guadalupanas de Cristo Rey, interviews with the author, Mexico City, Mexico. The same rule that I followed regarding my time with the brothers in Vermont also applies to my conversations with the sisters in Mexico, in that I will not identify them individually by name. I will mention that although I spoke with a number of sisters, both in Mexico City and in Cuernavaca, four specific sisters were designated from among the community to engage in formal interviews with me.

27. "Una nueva vida religiosa," 58.

28. Misioneras Guadalupanas de Cristo Rey, interviews with the author, Mexico City. The sisters expressed the same idea somewhat more poetically in their self-history, saying of their relationship with the brothers: "We ceased to have fathers; we found brothers." "Una nueva vida religiosa," 48.

29. Misioneras Guadalupanas de Cristo Rey, interviews with the author, Mexico City.

30. *Guadalupe Center*.

31. Misioneras Guadalupanas de Cristo Rey, interviews with the author, Mexico City.

32. The brothers are fond of saying self-deprecatingly that their initial instinct was to try to help the sisters by giving them money, until the sisters opened their eyes to the idea that true solidarity and a genuine *alianza*

could not be based on something so ephemeral, or frankly on something so inequitable.

33. Keck and Sikkink, *Activists beyond Borders*, 12.

34. *Saint Benedict's Rule*, 123 (chap. 53, para. 1).

35. See Bau, *This Ground Is Holy*, 10–12.

36. Ibid., 13.

37. Ibid., 9.

38. Ibid., 9.

39. The story was told in Clendinen, "Monastery Awaiting 5 Refugees."

40. Bau, *This Ground Is Holy*, 15.

41. Ibid.

42. Hammond, "Tell Your People." The newsletter is now available online, and all quotes from it will be cited from the online edition.

43. Ibid.

44. *Saint Benedict's Rule*, 45 (prologue, para. 1).

45. Benedictine Monks of Weston Priory, "Declaration of Public Sanctuary."

46. I have visited the priory many times and have stayed for periods of several days on three separate occasions. The brothers maintain a fairly strict regimen of silence at their monastery, so opportunities for informal conversation, although not nonexistent, are not plentiful. The community designated three brothers to engage with me in formal interviews, so I have held extensive conversations only with those three men.

47. See www.vamos.org.mx for further information on the organization; subsequent mentions are given in the text. Much of my knowledge of the organization comes from this website as well as my own visit in January 2009 to their centers in Cuernavaca, including informal conversation with staff members.

48. "Remembering Managua 1988."

49. Ibid.

50. Reagan, quoted in Boyd, "Reagan Terms Nicaraguan Rebels."

51. Weston Benedictine Monks, "Managua 2001."

52. Ibid.

53. This trip is recounted in Benedictine Monks of Weston Priory, "Life Together," Fall/Winter 2003.

54. These meetings are described in Benedictine Monks of Weston Priory, "Life Together," Spring/Summer 2002.

55. This process is the subject matter of *Guadalupe Center*.

56. The Faith and Hospitality Experience in a Latin American Context is heavily advertised on the priory's website. See www.westonpriory.org/mexico/index.html.

57. Ibid.

58. These quotes are taken from my contemporaneous notes of the conversations.

Chapter 5

1. Whitfield, *Paying the Price*, 83.

2. Donovan, quoted in DeChillo, "Maryknoll Pursues Its Vision."

3. Allen Hertzke credited the sisters with playing a powerful role in bringing about what he calls O'Neill's "effective opposition" to Reagan's contra war. *Representing God in Washington*, 78. However, he also argued that the Maryknollers' "mission work in Central America and elsewhere on the part of 'the poor' [had] fostered a critical attitude toward American influence abroad," more generally. Ibid., 37.

4. Keck and Sikkink, *Activists beyond Borders*.

5. Tarrow, *New Transnational Activism*.

6. Haas, "Epistemic Communities."

7. Healy, interview with the author, New York, NY.

8. Maryknoll Sisters of Saint Dominic, *Constitutions*, 5.

9. Alexander, interview with the author, San Salvador.

10. Misioneras Guadalupanas de Cristo Rey, interviews with the author, Mexico City, Mexico.

Bibliography

Abrams, Mike. "Kidnapped Nun Gives Eyewitness Account of Nicaraguan Scene." *South End* (Wayne State University, Detroit, MI), September 12, 1985.

Ahrari, Mohammed E. *Ethnic Groups and U.S. Foreign Policy.* New York: Greenwood Press, 1987.

Batliwala, Srilatha, and L. David Brown. *Transnational Civil Society: An Introduction.* Bloomfield, CT: Kumarian Press, 2006.

Bau, Ignatius. *This Ground Is Holy: Church Sanctuary and Central American Refugees.* Mahwah, NJ: Paulist Press, 1985.

Beirne, Charles. "Ordinary People Made Extraordinary," *Company* 171. www .companysj.com/v171/ordinary.html.

Benedict. *Saint Benedict's Rule.* Translated by Patrick Barry. Mahwah, NJ: Hidden Spring, 2004.

Benedictine Monks of Weston Priory. "A Declaration of Public Sanctuary." Press release, March 24, 1984. www.westonpriory.org/sanctuary/decla ration.html.

———. "Life Together in One Heart Chronicle." *Bulletin,* Fall/Winter 2003. www.westonpriory.org/bulletins/fw2003dd1.html.

———. "Life Together in One Heart Chronicle." *Bulletin,* Spring/Summer 2002. www.westonpriory.org/bulletins/ss2002b.html.

Berger, Peter, ed. *The De-secularization of the World: Resurgent Religion and World Politics.* Washington, DC: Ethics and Public Policy Center, 1999.

Berrigan, Daniel. *The Trial of the Catonsville Nine.* Toronto: Bantam Books, 1970.

Blanshard, Paul. *American Freedom and Catholic Power.* Boston: Beacon Press, 1949.

Boston Globe. "Slain Jesuits Endure as Focus for Activism." November 16, 1990.

Boyd, Gerald M. "Reagan Terms Nicaraguan Rebels 'Moral Equivalent of Founding Fathers.'" *New York Times,* March 2, 1985.

Brackley, Dean. "El Salvador: Personal Reflections Ten Years Later." *Jesuit Vocations.* www.jesuitvocations.com/marnyk/provinces/reflections/brack ley.html.

Brading, D. A. *Mexican Phoenix: Our Lady of Guadalupe; Image and Tradition across Five Centuries.* Cambridge: Cambridge University Press, 2003.

Breslin, Jimmy. "Nicaragua, Lady Liberty, and Crack." *New York Daily News*, June 29, 1986.

Brockman, James R. *Romero: A Life*. Maryknoll, NY: Orbis Books, 1989.

Byrnes, Timothy A. *Catholic Bishops in American Politics*. Princeton: Princeton University Press, 1991.

———. *Transnational Catholicism in Postcommunist Europe*. Lanham, MD: Rowman & Littlefield, 2001.

Clendinen, Dudley. "Monastery Awaiting 5 Refugees." *New York Times*, March 19, 1985.

Cogan, Mary de Paul. *Sisters of Maryknoll through Troubled Waters*. Freeport, NY: Books for Libraries Press, 1947.

Commission on the Truth for El Salvador. *From Madness to Hope: The 12-Year War in El Salvador*. 1993. www.usip.org/files/file/ElSalvador-Report.pdf.

DeChillo, Suzanne. "Maryknoll Pursues Its Vision of Mission." *New York Times*, March 31, 1985.

Documents of the 31st and 32nd General Congregations of the Society of Jesus. St. Louis: Institute of Jesuit Sources, 1977.

Doggett, Martha. *Death Foretold: The Jesuit Murders in El Salvador*. Washington: Georgetown University Press, 1993.

Dohen, Dorothy. *Nationalism and American Catholicism*. New York: Sheed and Ward, 1967.

Donovan, John F. *The Pagoda and the Cross: The Life of Bishop Ford of Maryknoll*. New York: Scribners, 1967.

Donziger, Steven. "Kidnapped American Nun Blames U.S. Government." United Press International, January 11, 1985.

Dullea, Georgia. "Memories of Death Linger at Maryknoll." *New York Times*, April 26, 1981.

Ellacuría, Ignacio. Commencement address, Santa Clara University, CA, June 1982. www.scu.edu/jesuits/ellacuria.html.

Ellison, Keith. Interview by Glenn Beck. CNN Headline News, November 14, 2006.

Everett, Melissa. *Bearing Witness, Building Bridges: Interviews with North Americans Living and Working in Nicaragua*. Philadelphia: New Society Publishers, 1985.

Ewald, Thomas. "Maryknoll Recounts Her Kidnapping." *Michigan Catholic*, September 13, 1985.

Farrell, John A. *Tip O'Neill and the Democratic Century*. Boston: Little, Brown, 2001.

Ford, Ita. *Here I Am Lord: The Letters and Writings of Ita Ford*. Edited by Jeanne Evans. Maryknoll, NY: Orbis Books, 2005.

Fraze, Barb. "Tales of Nicaraguan Torture Complicate U.S. Aid Issue." *The Dialog* (Wilmington, DE), March 22, 1985.

Ganss, George E., ed. *Ignatius Loyola: The Spiritual Exercises and Selected Works.* New York: Paulist Press, 1991.

Glazer, Nathan, and Daniel P. Moynihan. *Ethnicity.* Cambridge: Harvard University Press, 1975.

The Guadalupe Center: The Story of a Dream. DVD. Weston, VT: The Benedictine Foundation of the State of Vermont, 2006.

Haas, Peter M. "Epistemic Communities and International Policy Coordination." *International Organization* 46, no. 1 (Winter 1992): 1–35.

Hammond, John. *Benedictine Legacy of Peace: The Life of Abbot Leo A. Rudloff.* Weston, VT: Weston Priory, 2005.

———. "Tell Your People: The Plea of a Guatamalan Refugee Family." *Bulletin (Benedictine Monks of Weston Priory)*, March 2, 1983. www.weston priory.org/sanctuary/tellyour.html.

Healion, James V. "Nun Disagrees with Reagan on Nicaragua." *Journal-Courier* (New Haven, CT), July 9, 1985.

Herberg, Will. *Protestant, Catholic, Jew: An Essay in American Religious Sociology.* Garden City, NY: Doubleday, 1955.

Hertzke, Allen D. *Freeing God's Children: The Unlikely Alliance for Global Human Rights.* Lanham, MD: Rowman & Littlefield, 2004.

———. *Representing God in Washington: The Role of Religious Lobbies in the American Polity.* Knoxville: University of Tennessee Press, 1988.

Hillyer, Patricia. "Missionary Recalls Capture by Contras." *Denver Catholic Register*, August 14, 1985.

Huntington, Samuel P. "The Erosion of American National Interests." *Foreign Affairs*, Fall 1997, 28–49.

Kahin, George McTurnan. *Intervention: How America Became Involved in Vietnam.* New York: Knopf, 1986.

Katzenstein, Peter J., ed. *Between Power and Plenty: Foreign Economic Policies of Advanced Industrial States.* Madison: University of Wisconsin Press, 1978.

Keck, Margaret E., and Kathryn Sikkink. *Activists beyond Borders: Advocacy Networks in International Politics.* Ithaca: Cornell University Press, 1998.

Keohane, Robert O., and Joseph S. Nye. *Transnational Relations and World Politics.* Cambridge: Harvard University Press, 1973.

Kita, Bernice. *What Prize Awaits Us: Letters from Guatemala.* Maryknoll, NY: Maryknoll Sisters, 1988.

LaFeber, Walter. *Inevitable Revolutions: The United States in Central America.* New York: W. W. Norton, 1983.

Laskiewicz, Anne Marie. "Nun Contends U.S. Errs in Nicaragua." *Waterbury (CT) Sunday Republican,* June 23, 1985.

Laswell, Harold. *Politics: Who Gets What, When, How.* New York: McGraw Hill, 1936.

Lernoux, Penny. *Cry of the People: The Struggle for Human Rights in Latin America—the Catholic Church in Conflict with U.S. Policy.* New York: Penguin Books, 1980.

———. *Hearts on Fire: The Story of the Maryknoll Sisters.* Maryknoll, NY: Orbis Books, 1993.

Leukhardt, Bill. "Speakers Rap U.S. Aid to Contras." *Waterbury (CT) Republican,* May 12, 1985.

Lewis, Anthony. "Showing His Colors." *New York Times,* March 39, 1981.

Maria del Rey, Sister. *Her Name Is Mercy.* New York: Scribners, 1957.

Maryknoll Sisters of Saint Dominic. *Complementary Document.* Maryknoll, NY: Maryknoll Sisters of Saint Dominic, 1990.

———. *Constitutions.* Maryknoll, NY: Maryknoll Sisters of Saint Dominic, 1990.

———. *Mission Challenges.* Maryknoll, NY: Maryknoll Sisters of Saint Dominic, 1968.

———. *Searching and Sharing.* Maryknoll, NY: Maryknoll Sisters of Saint Dominic, 1968.

Mary Victoria, Sister. *Nun in Red China.* New York: McGraw-Hill, 1953.

Mathias, Charles McC., Jr. "Ethnic Groups and Foreign Policy." *Foreign Affairs,* Summer 1981, 975–98.

McLaughlin, Janice. *On the Frontline: Catholic Missions in Zimbabwe's Liberation War.* Harare, Zimbabwe: Baobob Books, 1996.

Mearsheimer, John J., and Stephen M. Walt. *The Israel Lobby and U.S. Foreign Policy.* New York: Farrar, Strauss and Giroux, 2007.

Melville, Thomas, and Marjorie Melville. *Guatemala: The Politics of Land Ownership.* New York: Free Press, 1971.

Meyer, Jean A. *The Cristero Rebellion: The Mexican People between Church and State 1926–1929.* Cambridge, UK: Cambridge University Press, 2008.

Montgomery, Tommie Sue. *Revolution in El Salvador: From Civil Strife to Civil Peace.* 2nd ed. Boulder, CO: Westview Press, 1995.

Nathanson, Rick. "American Nun Recounts Violence in Nicaragua." *Albuquerque Journal.*

Neal, Maria Augusta. *From Nuns to Sisters: An Expanding Vocation.* New London, CT: Twenty-third Publications, 1990.

Nevins, Albert J. *Adventures of Men of Maryknoll.* New York: Dodd, Mead, 1957.

New York Times. "Dispute in Salvador over Witness in Jesuit Case." December 11, 1989.

———. "Salvador Leader Links the Military to Priests' Killing." January 8, 1990.

———. "Witnesses in Jesuit Slayings Charge Harassment in U.S." December 18, 1989.

———. "Witness Links Killers of 6 Priests to Salvador's Armed Forces." November 28, 1989.

Noone, Judith M. *The Same Fate as the Poor.* Maryknoll, NY: Maryknoll Sisters Publications, 1984.

O'Donovan, Leo. "Martyrdom and Mercy." *Washington Post,* November 19, 1989.

O'Hare, Joseph. "In Solidarity with the Slain Jesuits of El Salvador." *America,* December 16, 1989, 443–46.

Ostling, Richard. "Those Beleaguered Maryknollers." *Time,* July 6, 1981.

Pattee, Sarah. "A Nun Brings a Message of Protest from Nicaragua." *San Antonio Light,* September 20, 1985.

"Remembering Managua 1988: The Wounded Children." *Bulletin (Benedictine Monks of Weston Priory),* 2001. www.westonpriory.org/nicaragua/nic3b.html

Risse-Kappen, Thomas. "Bringing Transnational Relations Back In: Introduction." In *Bringing Transnational Relations Back In: Non-state Actors, Domestic Structures, and International Institutions,* edited by Thomas Risse-Kappen, 3–33. New York: Cambridge University Press, 1995.

Robert, Dana L. *American Women in Mission: History of Their Thought and Practice.* Macon, GA: Mercer University Press, 1997.

Romero, Oscar. *Voice of the Voiceless: The Four Pastoral Letters and Other Statements.* With an introduction by Jon Sobrino. Maryknoll, NY: Orbis Books, 1985.

Rudolph, Susanne H., and James Piscatori. *Transnational Religion and Fading States.* Boulder, CO: Westview, 1996.

Ryall, David. "The Catholic Church as a Transnational Actor." In *Non-state Actors in World Politics,* edited by Daphne Josselin and William Wallace, 41–58. New York: Palgrave, 2001.

Second Vatican Council. *Pastoral Constitution on the Church in the Modern World.* In *The Documents of Vatican II,* edited by Walter M. Abbott and Joseph Gallagher. New York: Guild Press, 1966.

Seib, Gerald. "Catholic and Other U.S. Church Groups Oppose Reagan's Hard-line Policy on Central America." *Wall Street Journal,* December 12, 1983.

Shain, Yossi. "Multicultural Foreign Policy." *Foreign Policy,* Fall 1995, 69–88.

Skillicorn, David. *With One Heart: The Benedictine Monks of Weston Priory.* DVD/VHS. Weston, VT: Benedictine Foundation of the State of Vermont, 2003.

Smidt, Corwin E., Lyman A. Kellstedt, and James L. Guth. "The Role of Religion in American Politics: Explanatory Theories and Associated Analytical and Measurement Issues." In *The Oxford Handbook of Religion and American Politics,* edited by Corwin E. Smidt, Lyman A. Kellstedt, and James L. Guth, 3–42. Oxford: Oxford University Press, 2009.

Sobrino, Jon. *Witnesses to the Kingdom: The Martyrs of El Salvador and the Crucified Peoples.* Maryknoll, NY: Orbis Books, 2003.

Tarrow, Sidney. *The New Transnational Activism.* New York: Cambridge University Press, 2005.

Taubman, Philip. "The Speaker and His Sources on Latin America." *New York Times,* September 12, 1984.

Truman, David B. *The Governmental Process: Political Interests and Public Opinion.* New York: Knopf, 1951.

"Una nueva vida religiosa es posible: Historia de las Misioneras Guadalupanas de Cristo Rey, OSB." Unpublished manuscript. 2007.

Walsh, Frank. *Sin and Censorship: The Catholic Church and the Motion Picture Industry.* New Haven: Yale University Press, 1996.

Waltz, Kenneth. *Theory of International Politics.* Reading, MA: Addison-Wesley, 1979.

Walzer, Michael. *Toward a Global Civil Society.* Providence, RI: Berghahn Books, 1997.

Washington Post. "Justice Disserved in the Jesuit Murders." October 14, 1991.

Weston Benedictine Monks. "Managua 2001: A Very Different Journey." Winter 2001. www.westonpriory.org/nicaragua/nic01.html.

Whitfield, Teresa. *Paying the Price: Ignacio Ellacuría and the Murdered Jesuits of El Salvador.* Philadelphia: Temple University Press, 1995.

Wilcox, Clyde, and Carin Larson. *Onward Christian Soldiers: The Religious Right in American Politics.* 3rd ed. Boulder, CO: Westview Press, 2006.

Winter, Janice. "Faith in the War Zone: Maryknoll Sister Tells of Life in Nicaragua." *The Record* (Louisville, KY), August 15, 1985.

Yehle, Monica Ann. "A Sister with Spunk." *Catholic New York,* January 17, 1985.

Index

accompaniment, concept of, 70–71, 76, 79–80

Activists beyond Borders (Keck and Sikkink), 23, 127

Adams, Brock, 58

Adventures of the Men of Maryknoll (Nevins), 75

Ahrari, Mohammed, 17–22, 58, 82

Allende, Salvador, 89

American Freedom and Catholic Power (Blanshard), 84

anticommunism: Cold War–era Catholic lobby and, 83–85; Maryknoll sisters and, 84–85, 91–92, 103; Reagan's narrative of communist threat in Central America, 91–92, 103

Arco Iris de Alianza. *See* Benedictines' transnational network and the Arco Iris de Alianza

Arrupe, Pedro, 44–45, 48, 65–66, 70

assimilation, 18–20

Association of Jesuit Colleges and Universities (AJCU), 39, 51, 53–54

Atlacatl Battalion of the Salvadoran Army, 29, 49–50, 60–61

Azuela, Fernando, 35

The Bamboo Curtain (film), 76–77

Basilica of Our Lady of Guadalupe (Mexico City), 119–20, 144

Bau, Ignatius, 129–30

Beirne, Charles, 66; and Ellacuría, 30, 36; on Jesuit process of discernment, 34, 35; lobbying Congress to forgive UCA's debt, 54; and Moakley Commission, 55; and

Salvadoran government investigation/trial of the Jesuit case, 51, 55, 61; and Santa Clara University, 30–31, 35; volunteer replacement team sent to UCA, 30–31, 33–34, 35–37

Benavides, Guillermo Alfredo, 60, 61, 67

Benedictine Abbey of Tournay, France, 141

Benedictine brothers of the Weston Priory, 107, 112–17, 158; autonomy and structural relationship to Benedictine Confederation, 112–13, 117–18; and Guadalupe Center, 143–45; Guatemala trip (2003), 140; monastic restoration centered on prayer and work, 113–15, 121, 132, 177n11; music of, 115–16, 124, 126, 133, 143, 145, 177n16; new focus and relationship to outside world, 123–24, 149; newsletter and website, 133; Nicaragua trips (1988 and 2001), 137–40; political access, 127–28; providing sanctuary for Guatemalan refugees, 129–33, 140, 161; receptivity to the Alianza, 116–17, 134, 177n18; reverse mission, 124, 125–26, 132, 133; rural Vermont monastery, 112–15, 150; transnational network, 122–23, 129–33, 137–40, 143–45; transnational network and the Arco Iris de Alianza, 122–23, 149. *See also* Benedictines' transnational network and the Arco Iris de Alianza

accompaniment, 70–71, 76, 79–80; as missioners, 6, 12–13, 70–71, 72–81; motherhouse in Ossining, New York, 68, 77, 93; periodical *The Field Afar*, 74, 83, 92; process of recognition as religious congregation, 74–75; and social revolutions of 1960s and 1970s, 77–81; and Vatican II reforms, 77–79; and World War II, 85, 87. *See also* Maryknoll Sisters of Saint Dominic and transnational political engagement
Maryknoll Sisters of Saint Dominic and transnational political engagement, 1–2, 9–10, 68–105, 153–54, 160; alternative narrative of Central American wars, 91–92; and anticommunism, 84–85, 91–92, 103; and anti-Vietnam War movement, 94–96; apolitical nature of early missions, 81–82, 86–87, 89; calculating their political effectiveness in changing US policy, 154; and Central American civil wars of the 1980s, 82–92; congressional testimony, 69–70, 96–101, 154, 160; counterbalancing demonization of the Sandinistas, 102–4; critics of the politicization of the mission, 87, 90, 103–4; dual political identities, 20, 72, 73, 83; early Chinese missions, 83–85; early encounters with politics, 81–88; expansive definition of "ours," 82, 86–88, 91, 97, 105; homogeneity/diversity, 21; influence on Tip O'Neill, 98–100, 154, 160, 164; "Melville incident," 95–96; as missioners, 6, 12–13, 70–71, 72–81; the murders of Ford and Clarke in El Salvador, 88–92, 104, 153; oppositional activism, 86–87; political access and credibility, 98–100, 127; political activism motivated

by communal identification and solidarity, 82, 86–88, 91, 154; politicization in the field, 86–87; and Reagan's aggressive foreign policy in Central America, 90, 91–92; reverse mission, 24, 69–72, 92–105, 126, 132, 149, 154; transnational political engagement commensurate with internal structures and communal commitments, 11–12, 26, 104–5, 126, 132, 149, 153–54, 160, 163–64; and US policy supporting contras against Sandinistas in Nicaragua, 1, 69–72, 83–88, 90–92, 97–105, 137–38, 153–54, 174n2, 175n62; as "voice for the voiceless," 96–98, 104–5; World Awareness Programs, 93
Mathias, Charles, 15–16
McGovern, Jim, 54–55
McLaughlin, Janice, 96
Mearsheimer, John, 17
Melville, Marjorie Bradford, 94–96, 129
Melville, Thomas, 94–96, 129
Mendoza, Yusshy, 60
Mexico: Cristo Rey and history of Catholic Church under Ley Calles, 120; the Guadalupe Center in Cuernavaca, 1, 106–7, 124–25, 136, 142–47, 149, 150, 155, 161; Our Lady of Guadalupe and Mexican Catholicism, 119–20; Vamos! network in Cuernavaca, 133–36. *See also* Benedictine sisters of Las Misioneras Guadalupanas de Cristo Rey (the Guadalupanas)
Las Misioneras Guadalupanas de Cristo Rey. *See* Benedictine sisters of Las Misioneras Guadalupanas de Cristo Rey (the Guadalupanas)
Moakley, Joseph, 54–56, 59, 60
mobility, principle of, 32–34